I0488508

SUPER CUTE FAIRIES & MERMAIDS

&

CREATURES OF THE SEA

COLORING BOOK

SUPER CUTE FAIRIES & MERMAIDS

Fantasy Coloring Book

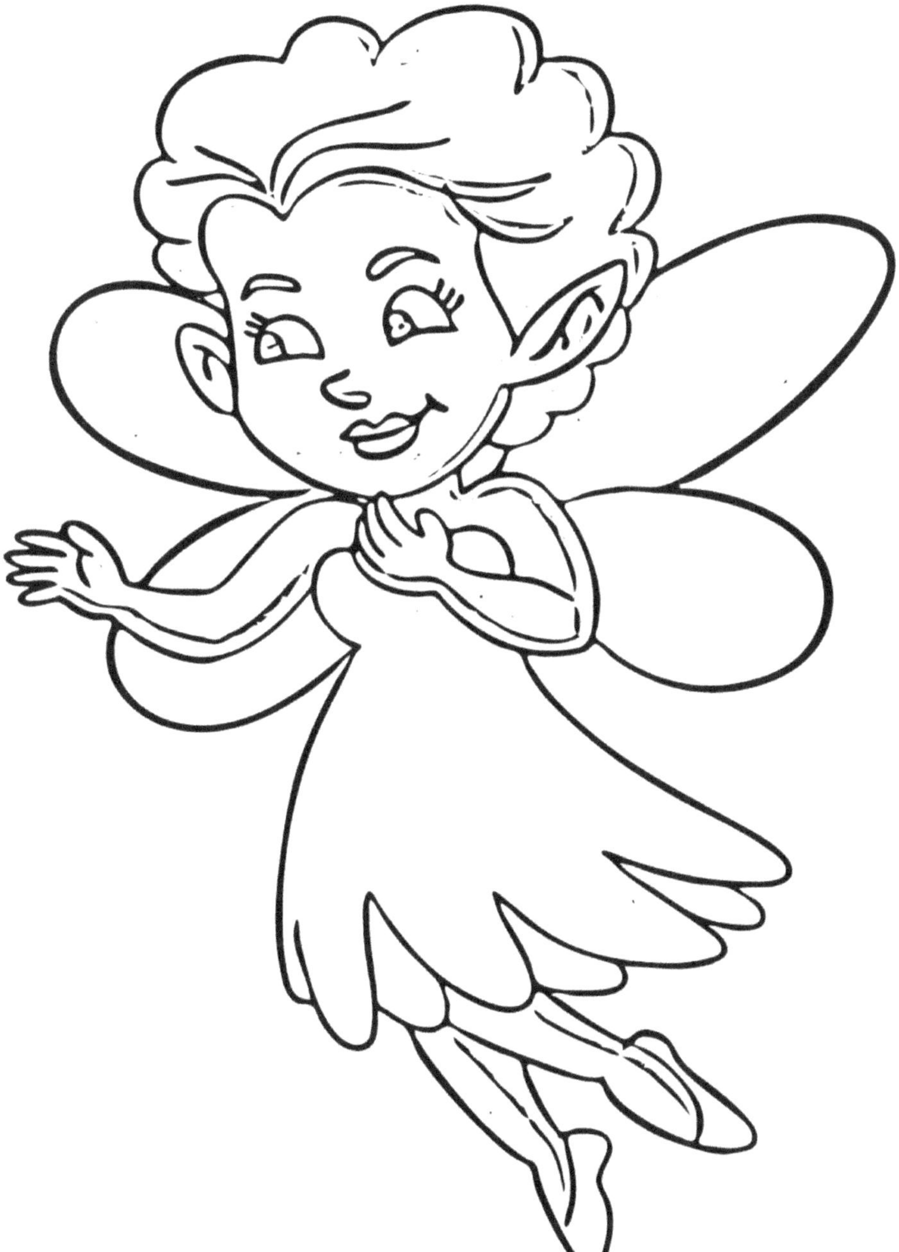

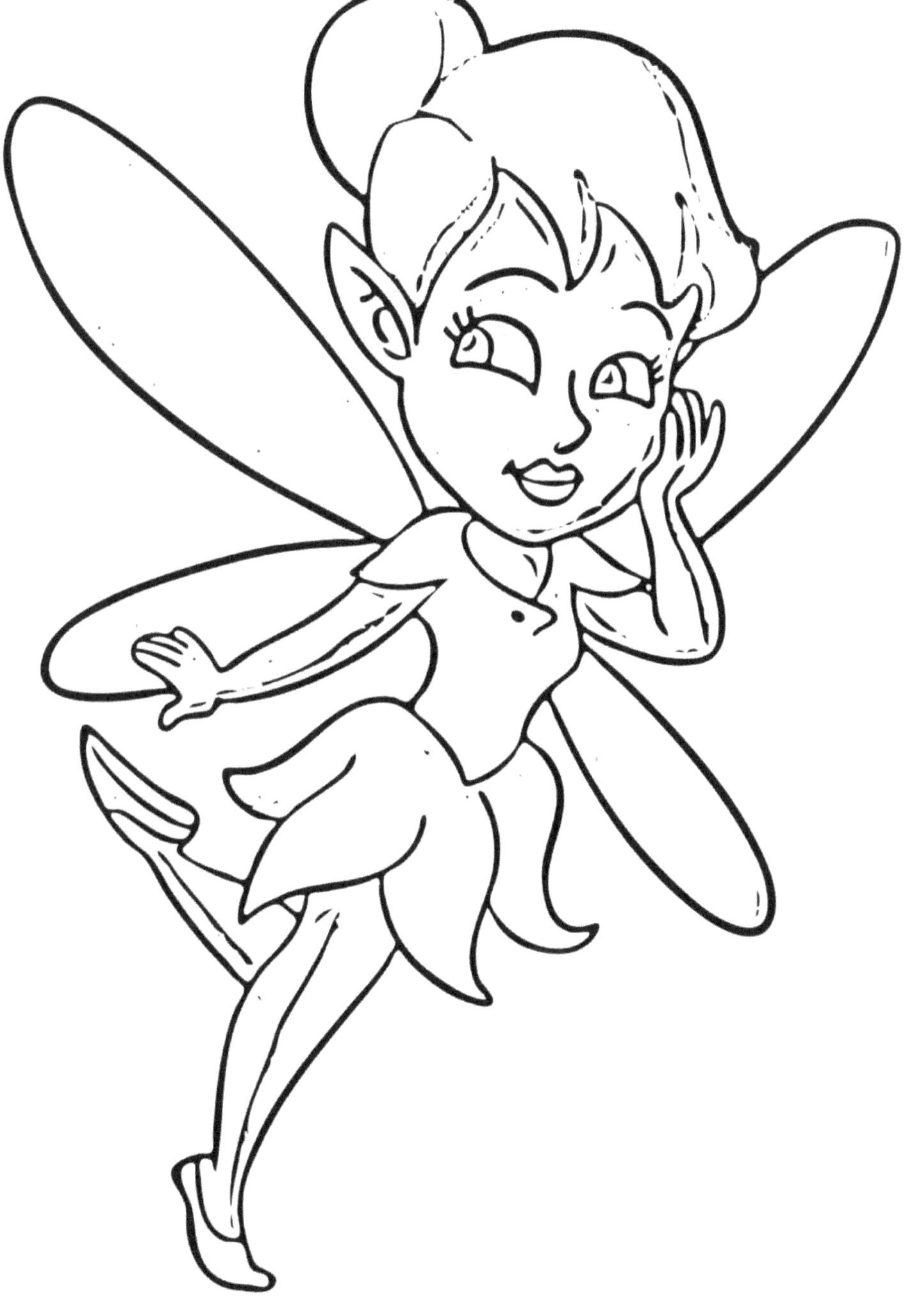

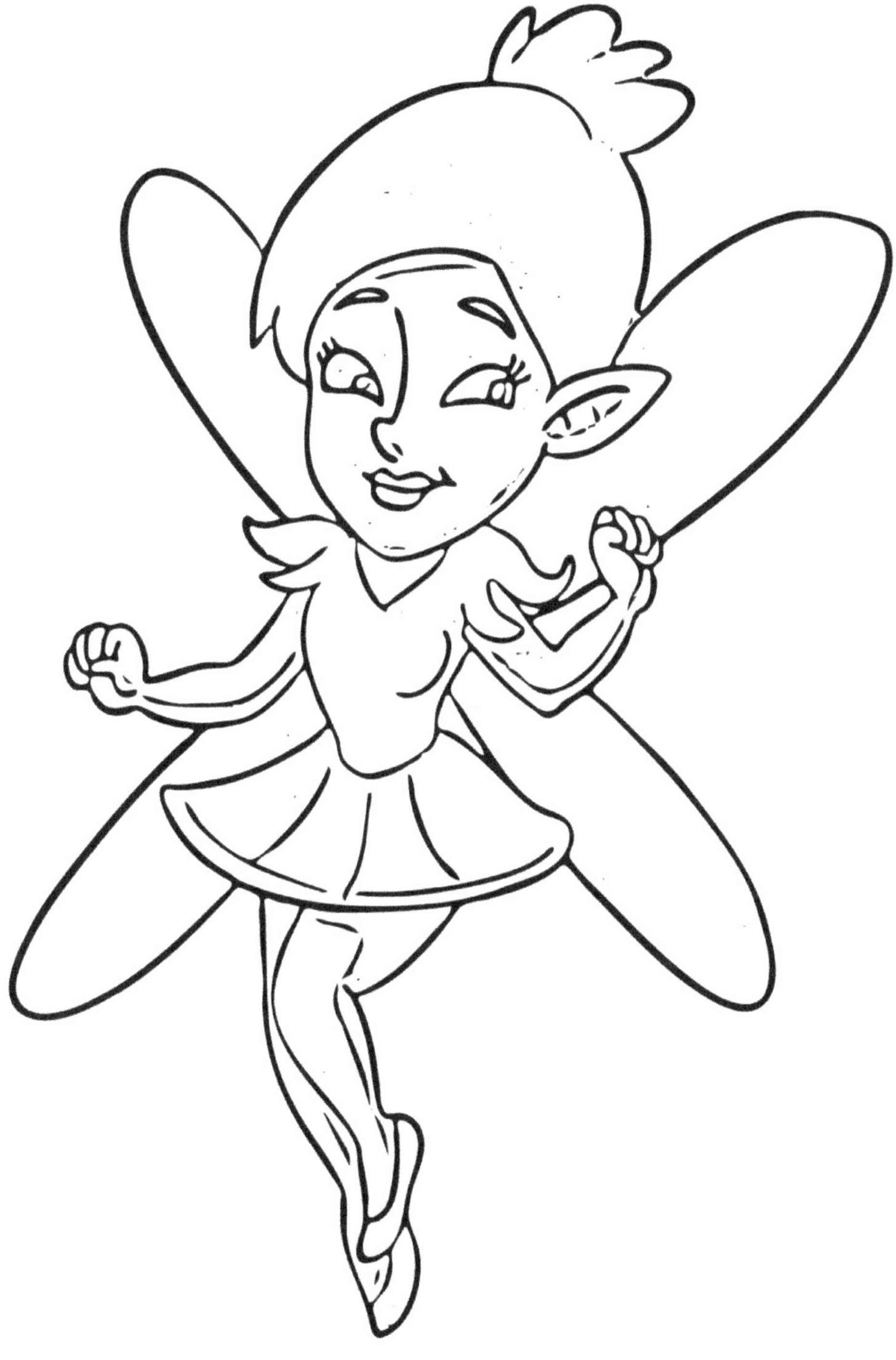

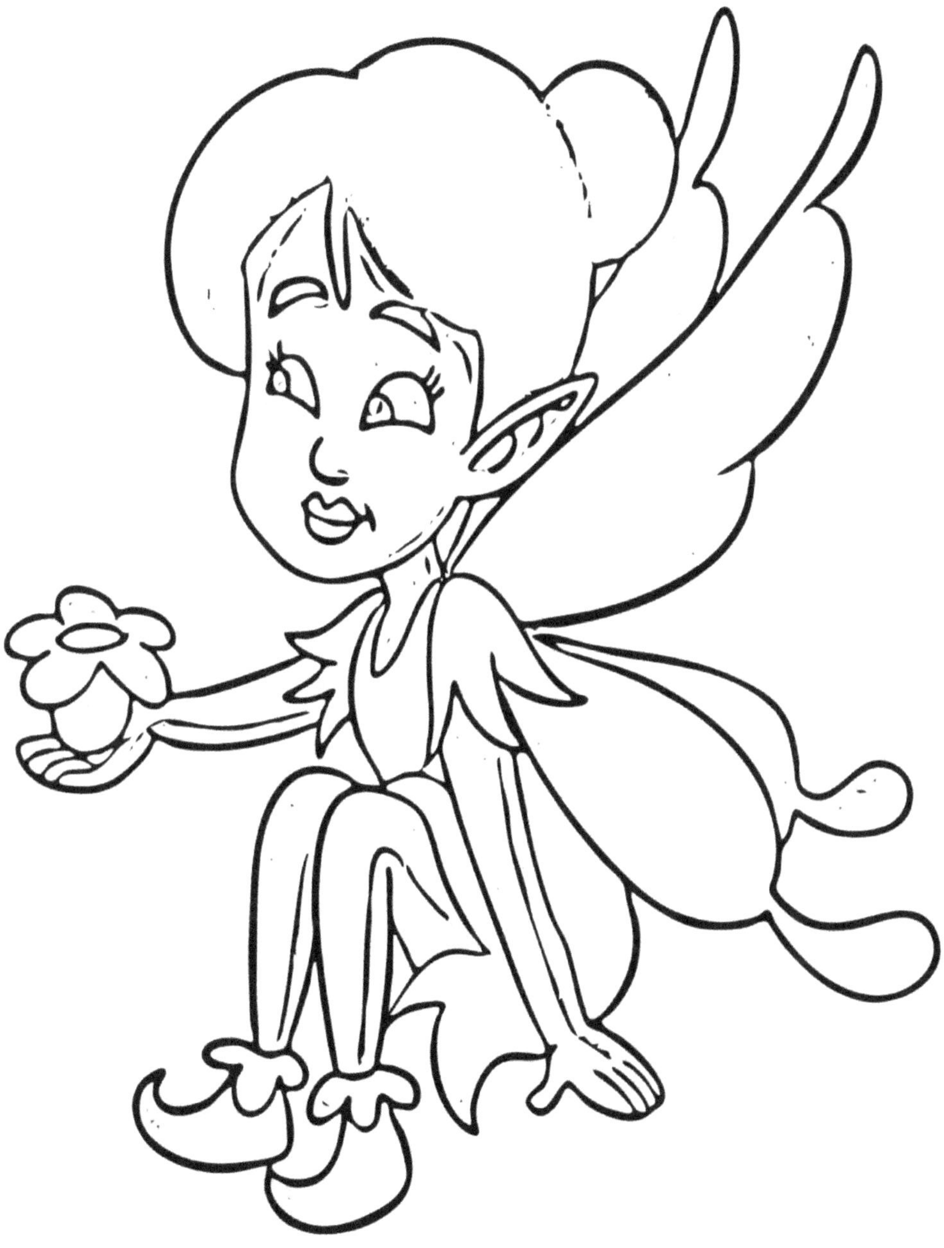

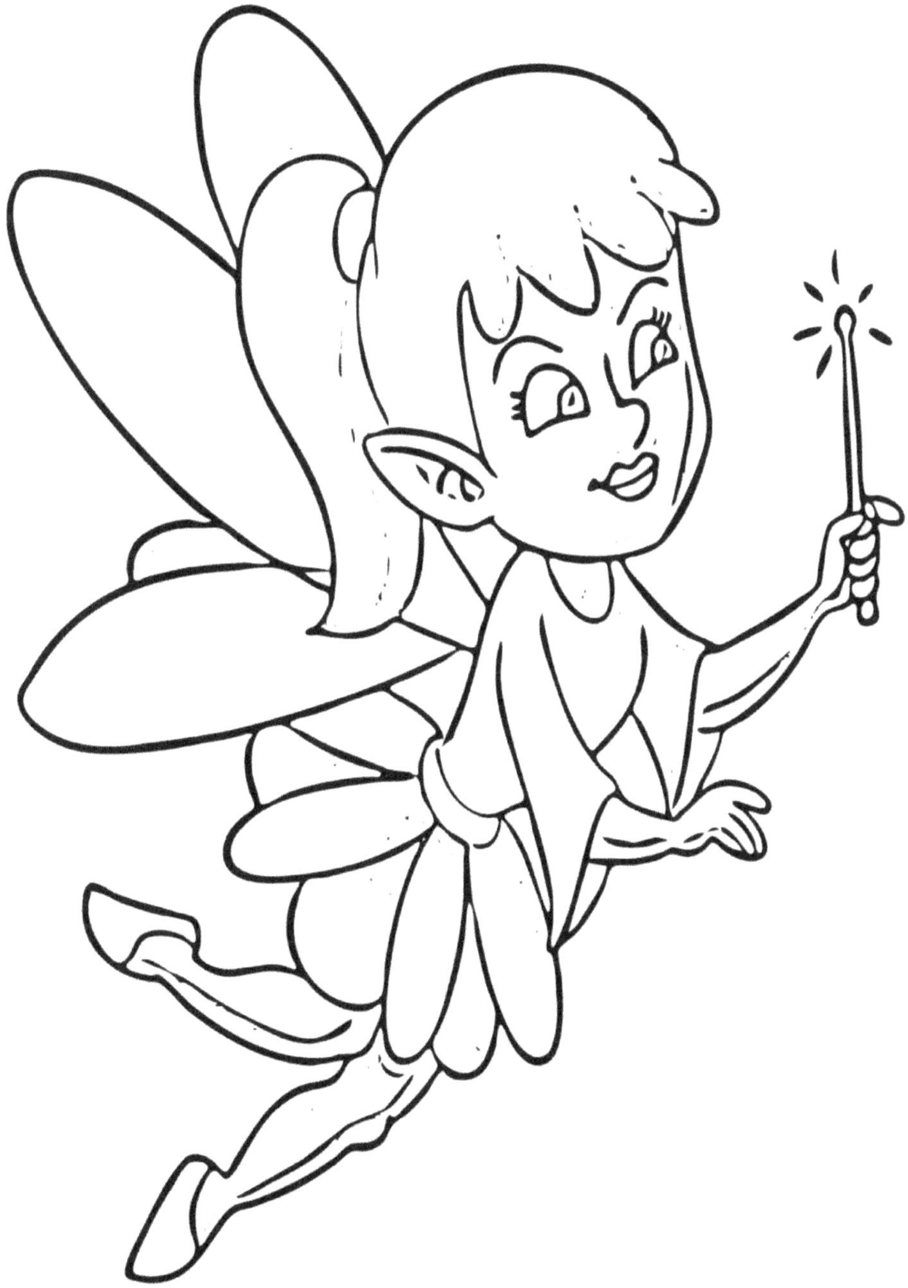

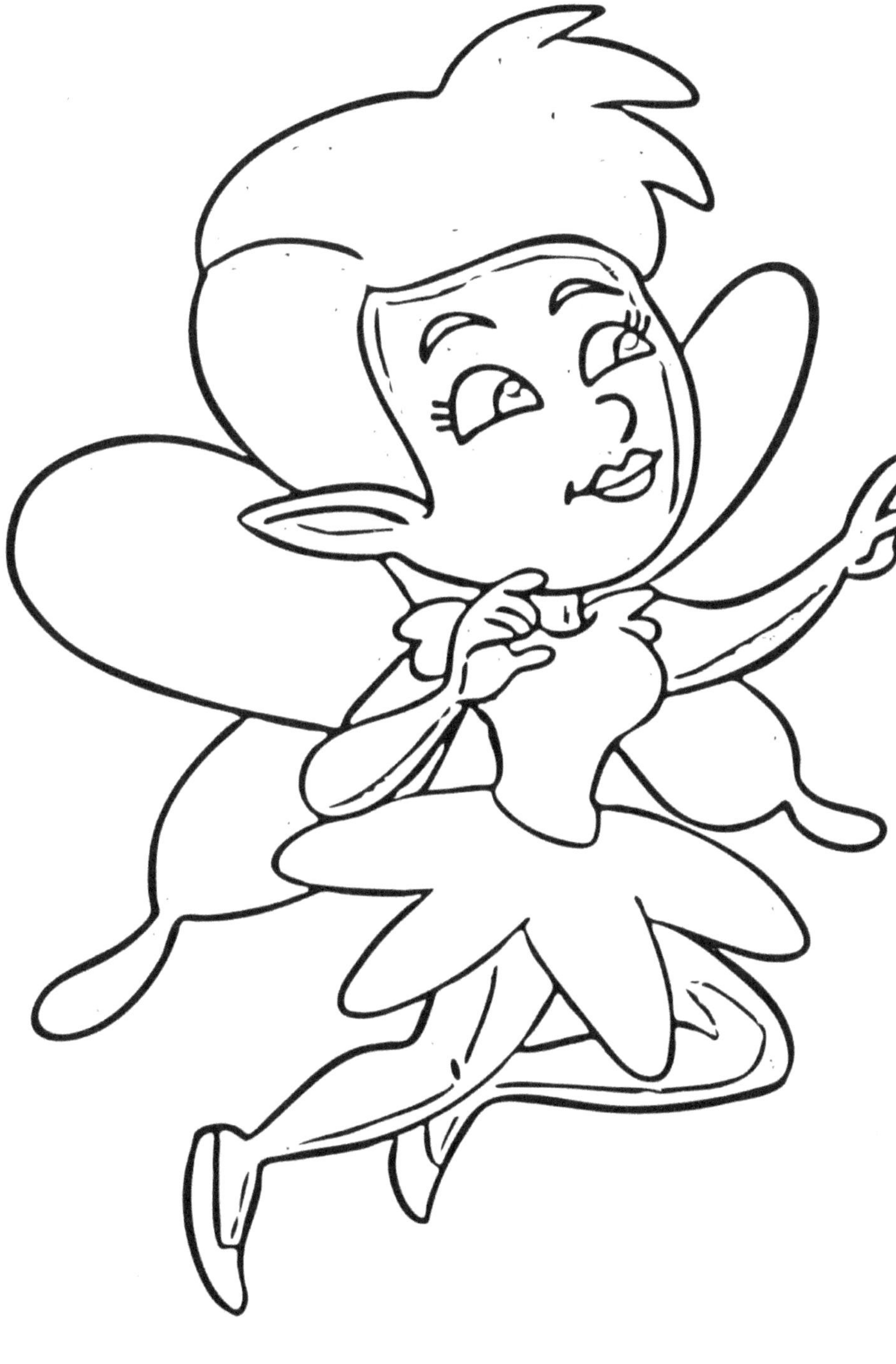

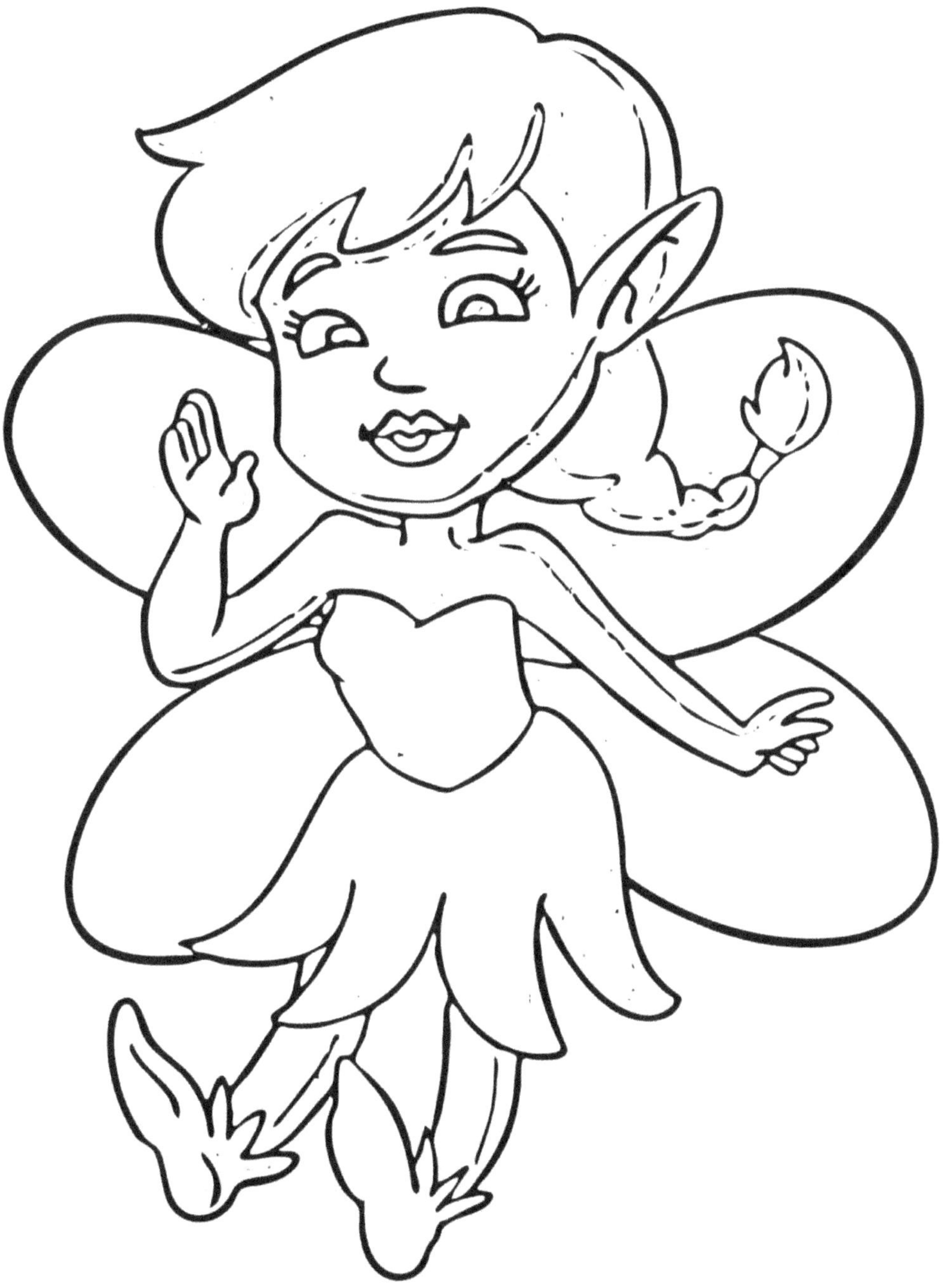

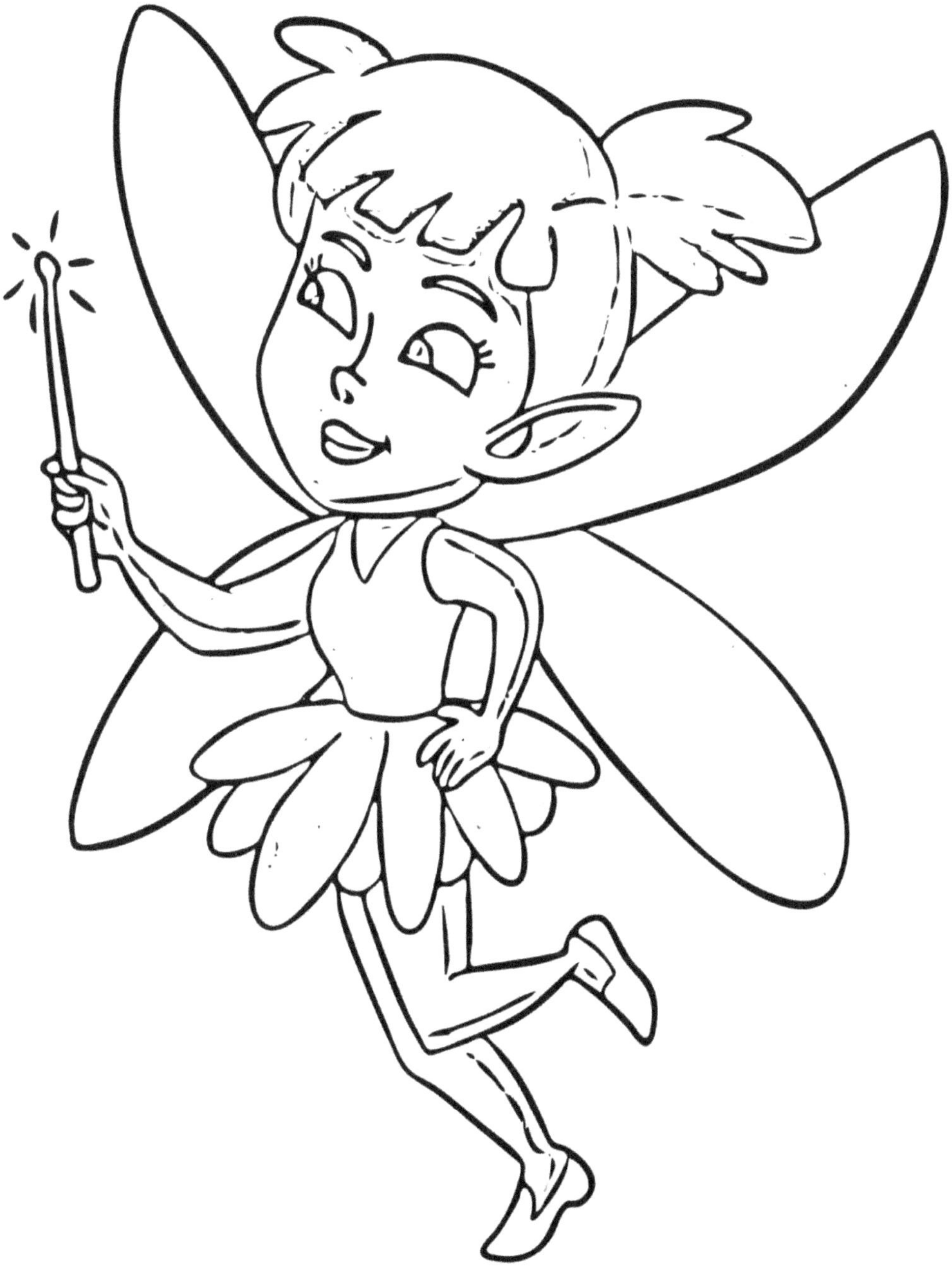

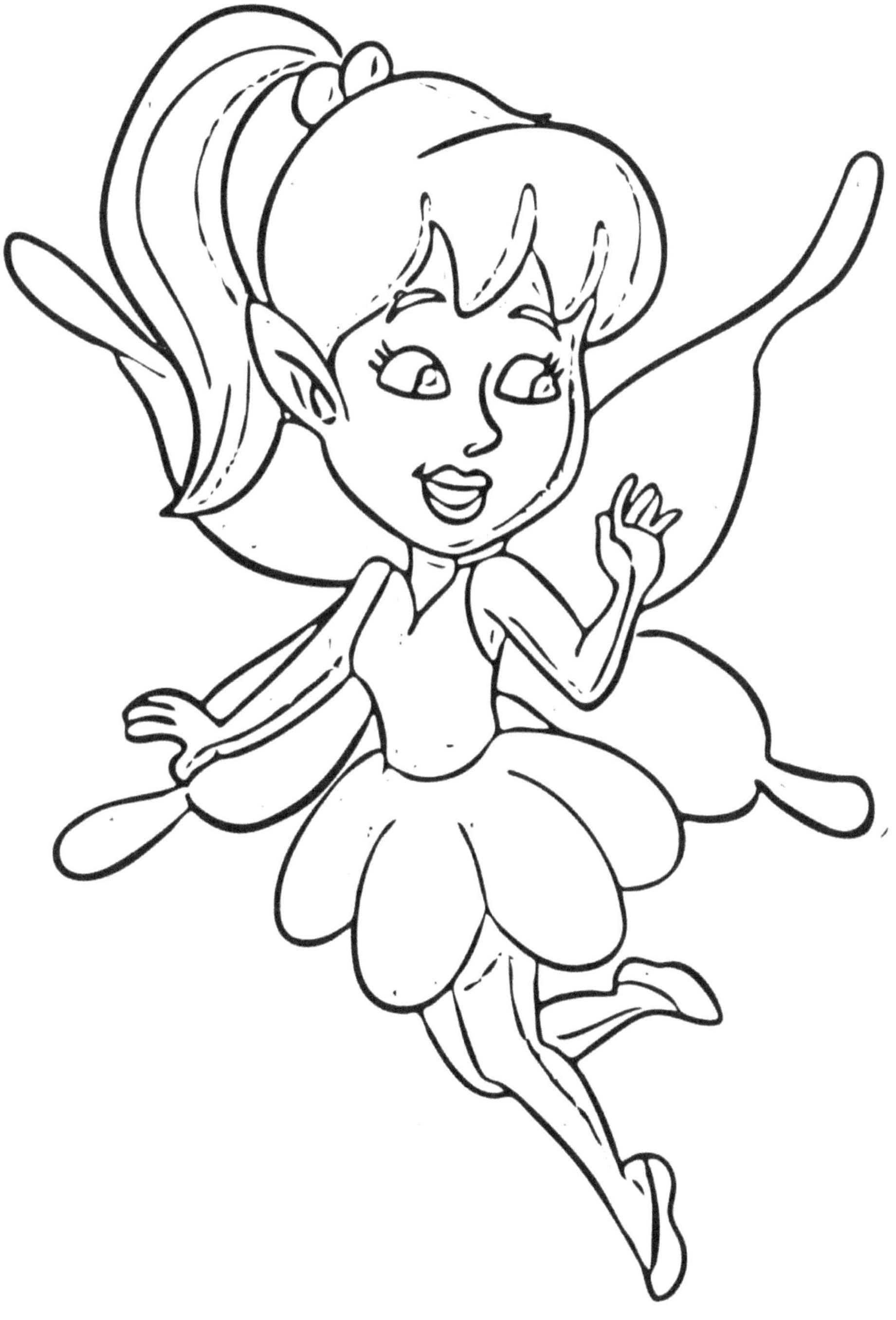

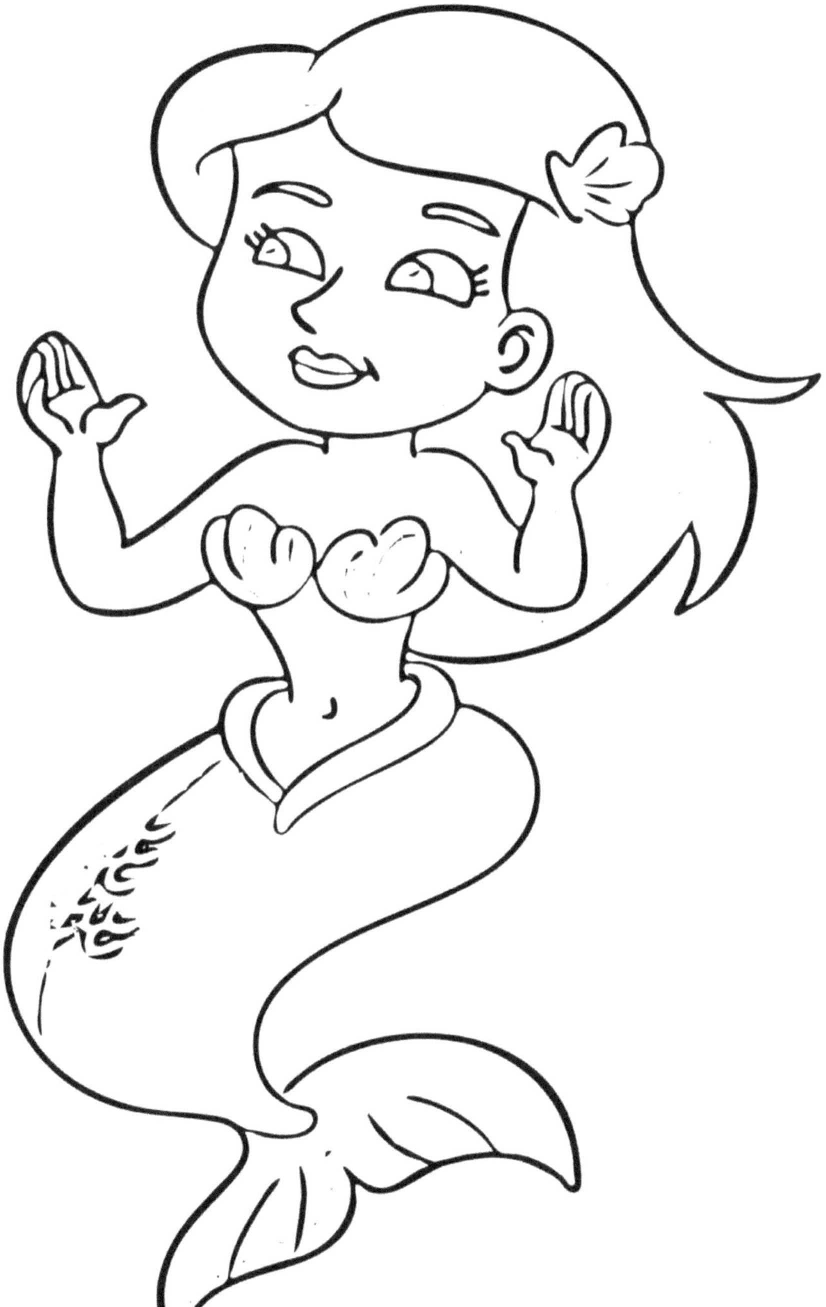

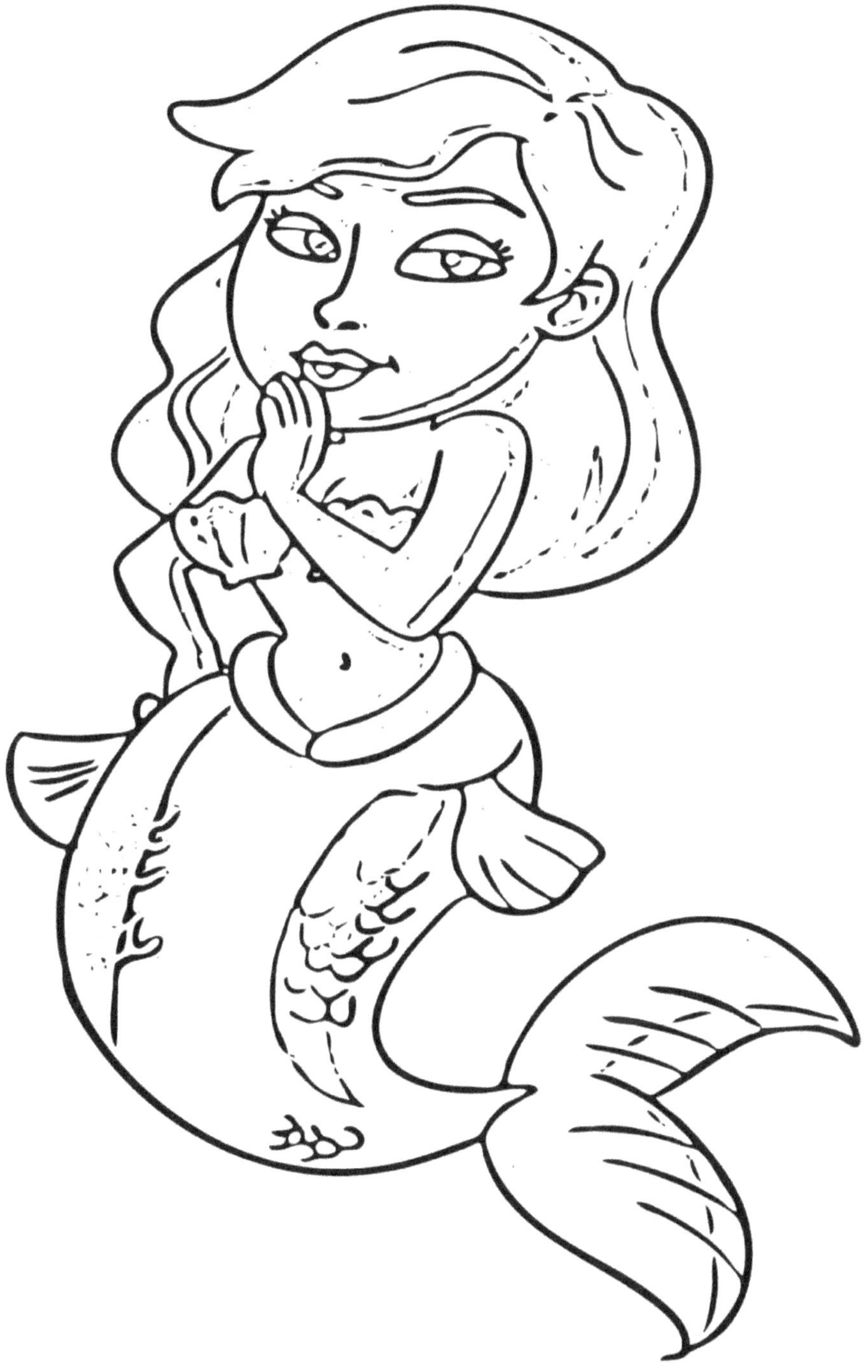

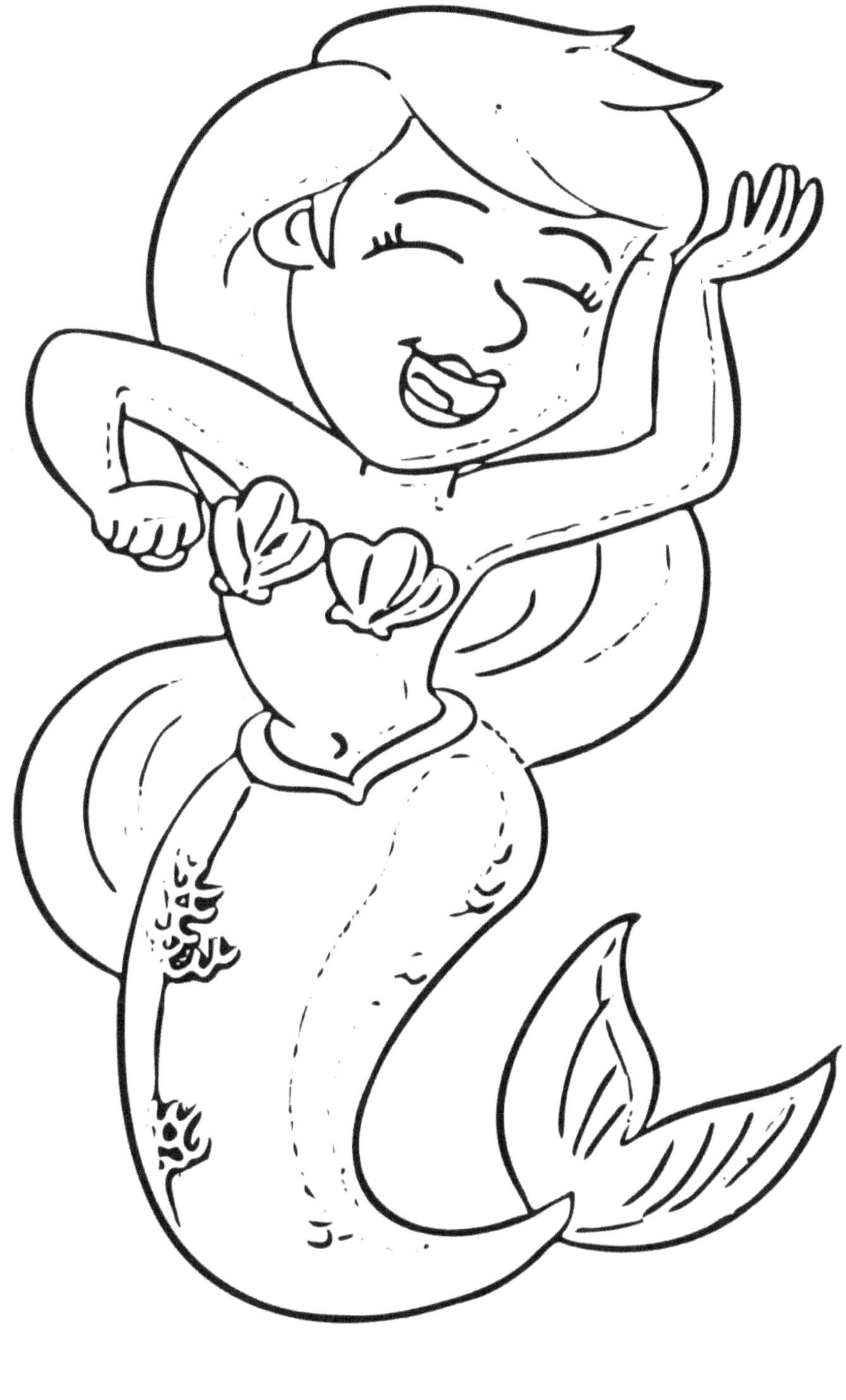

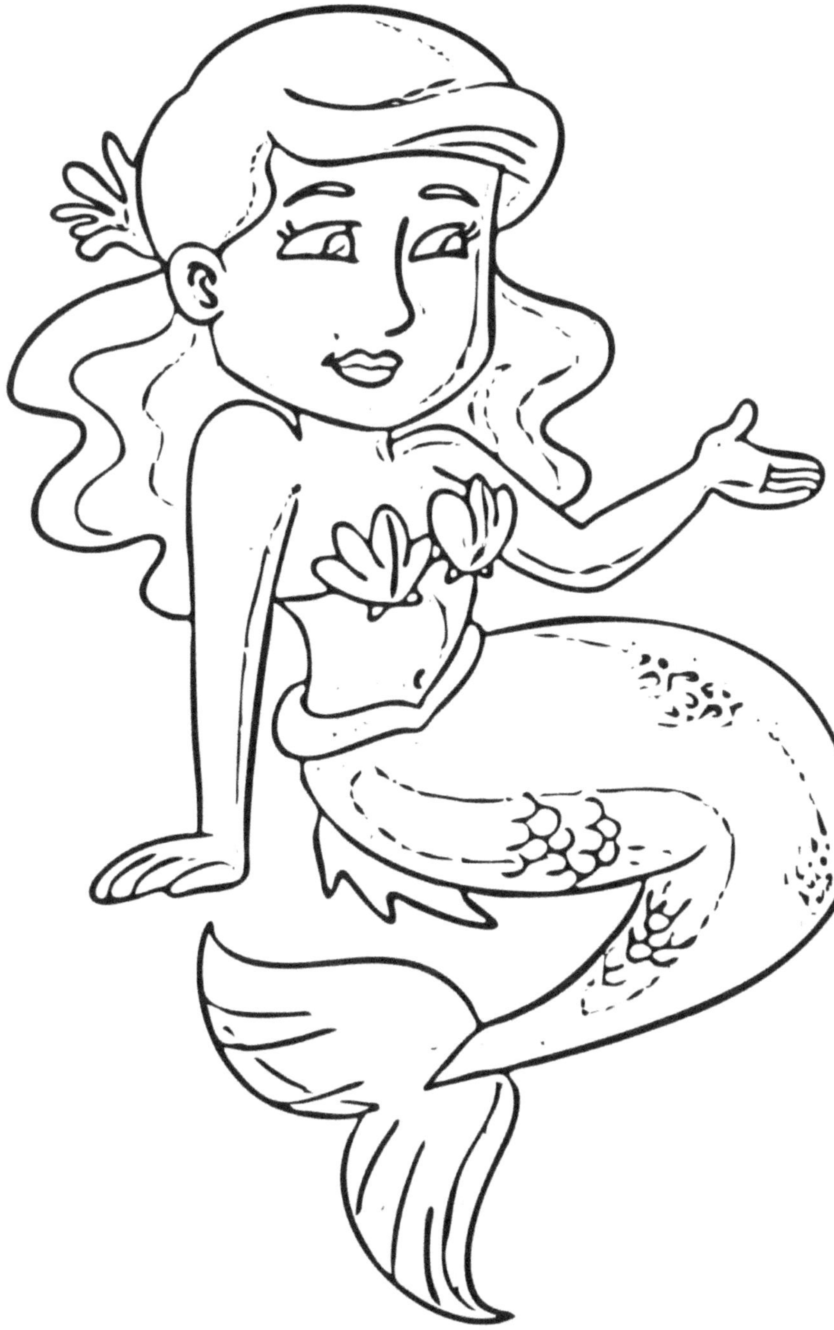

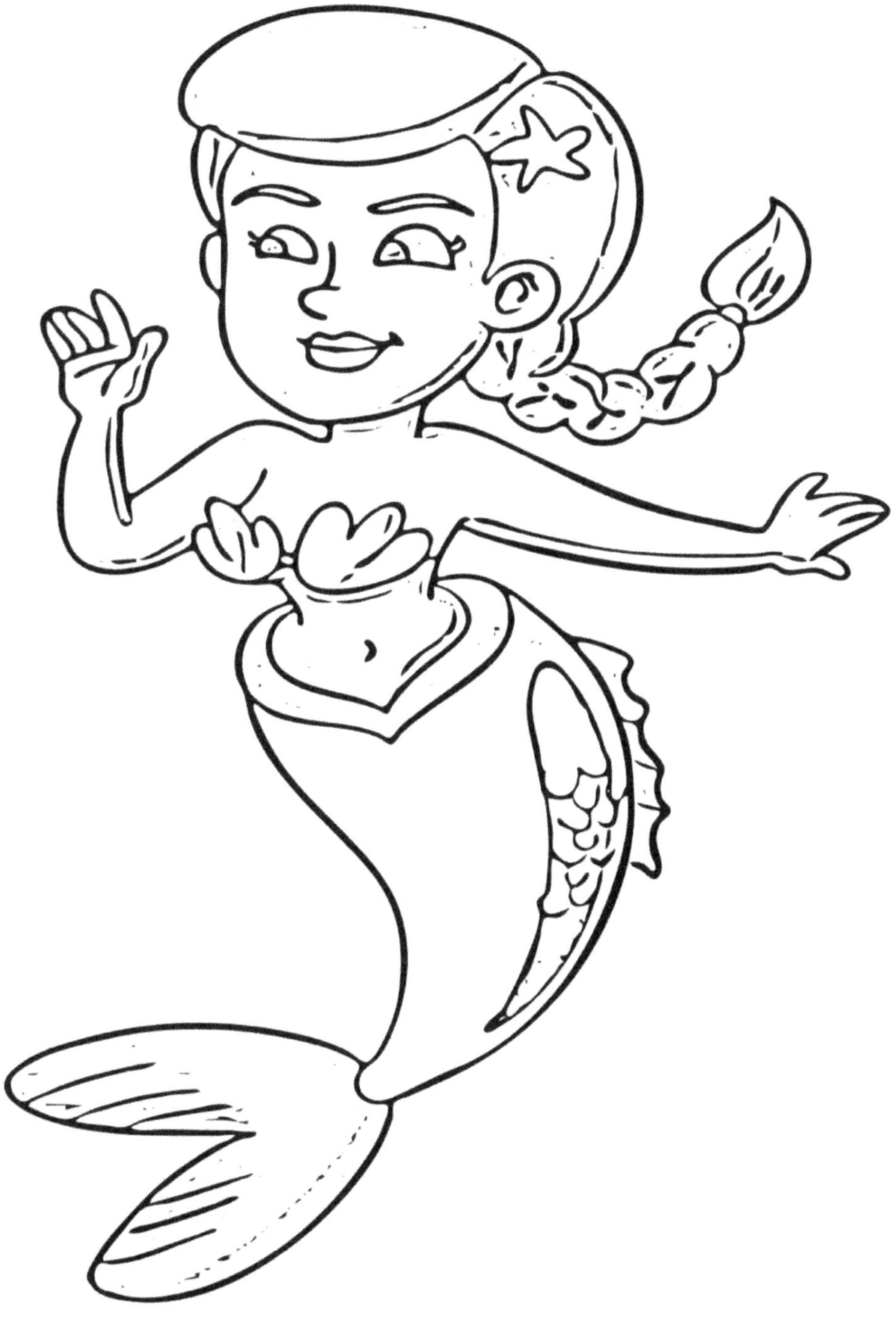

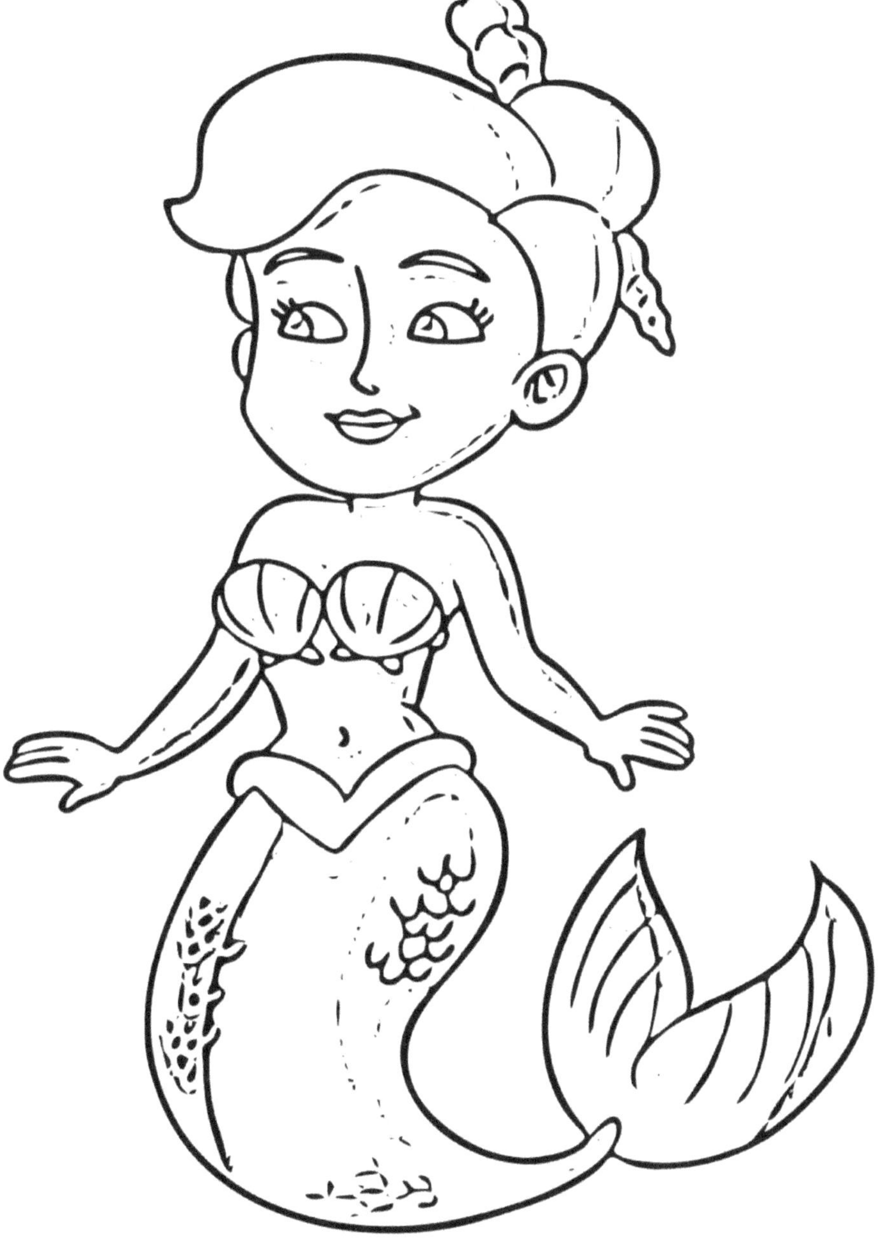

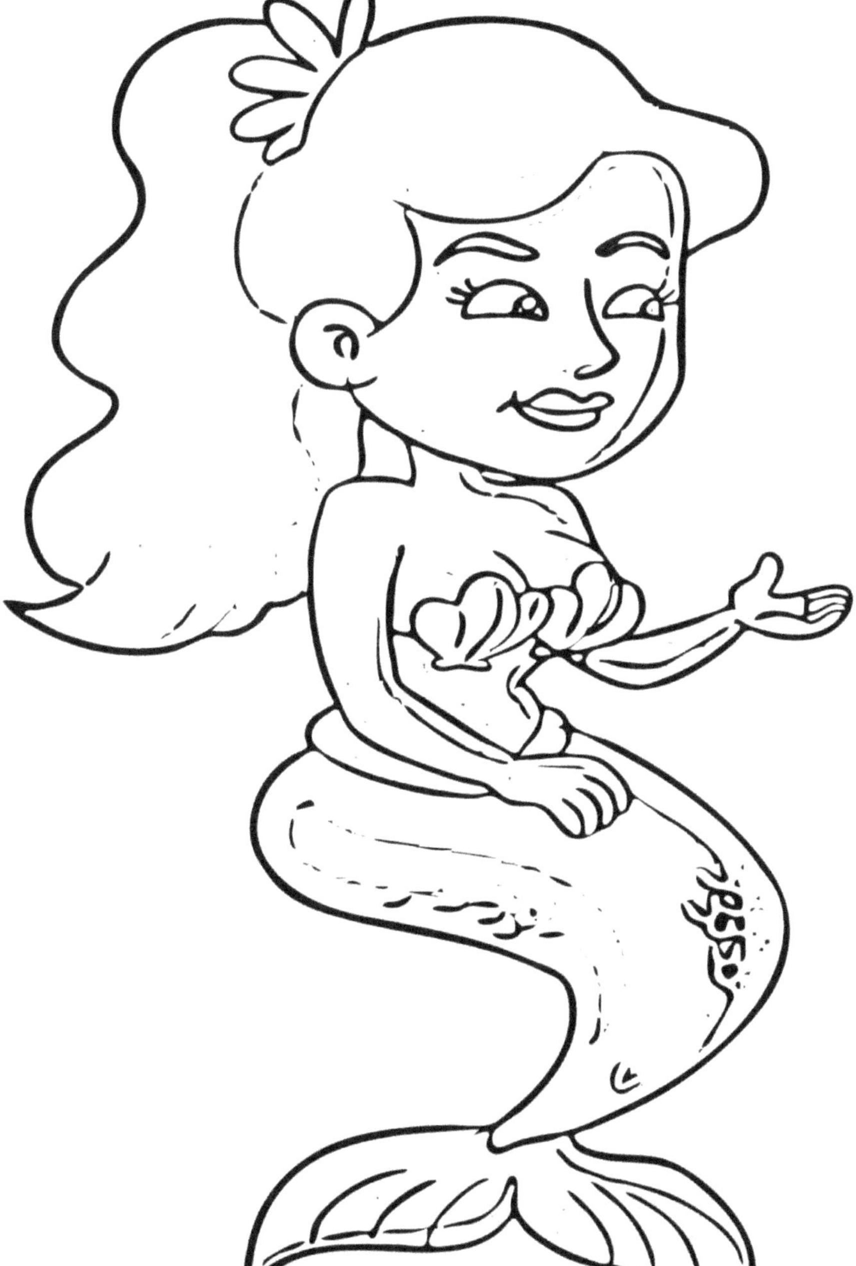

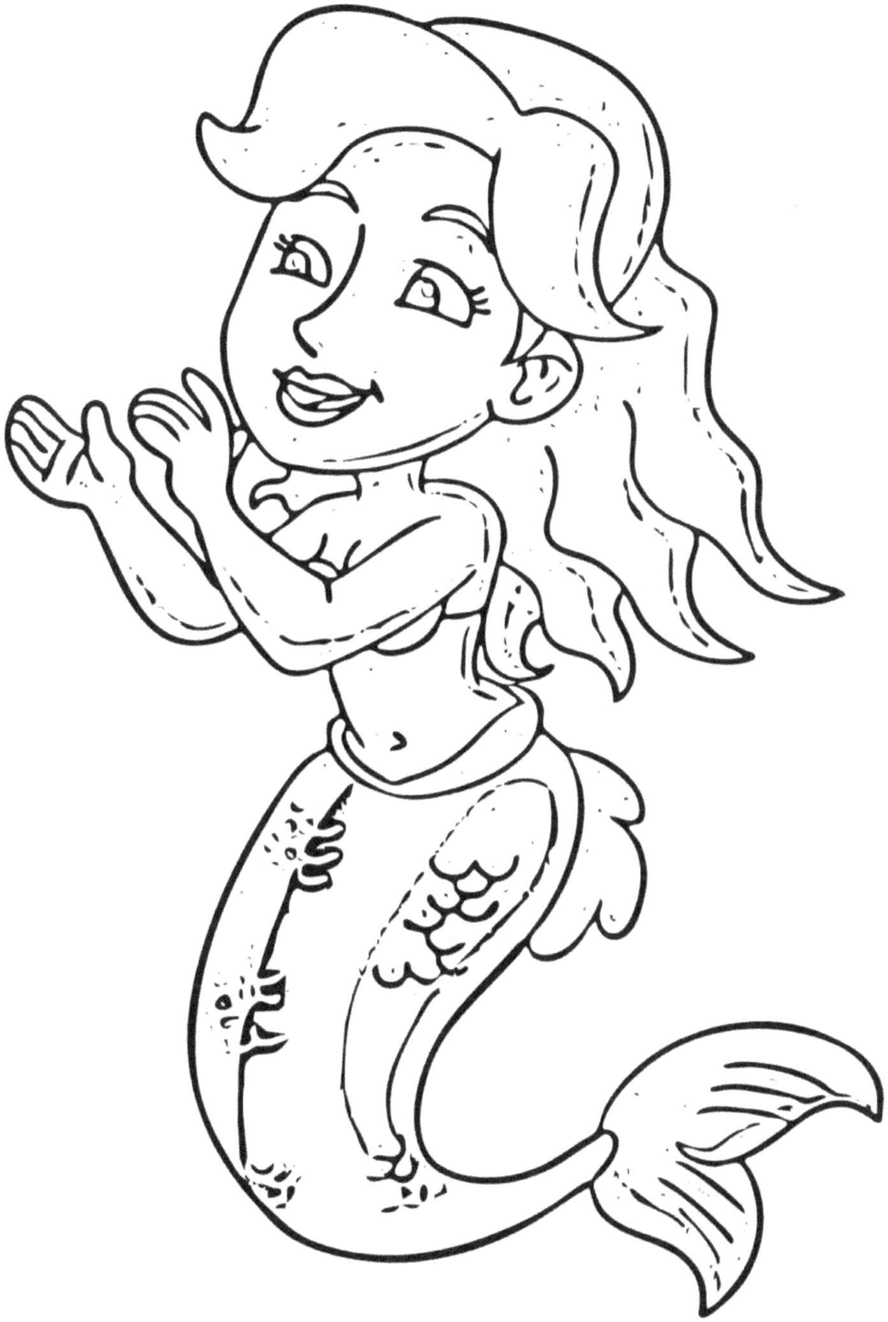

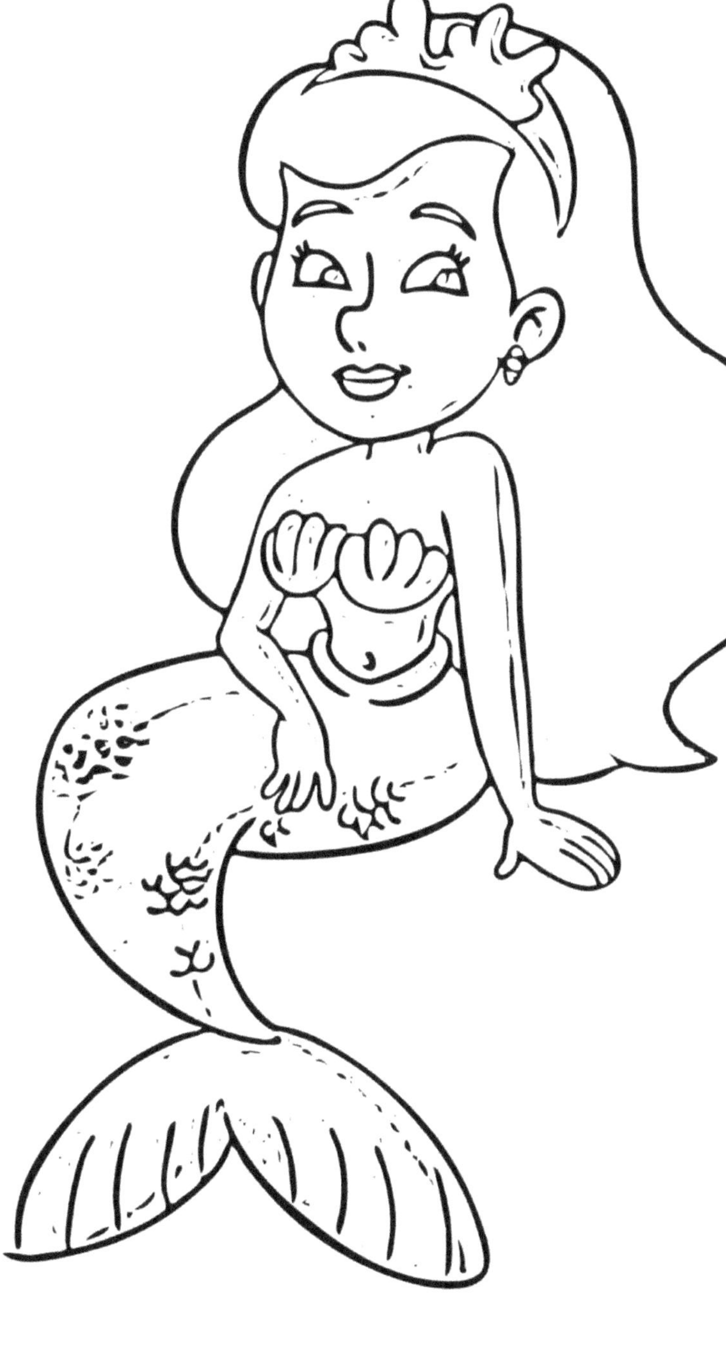

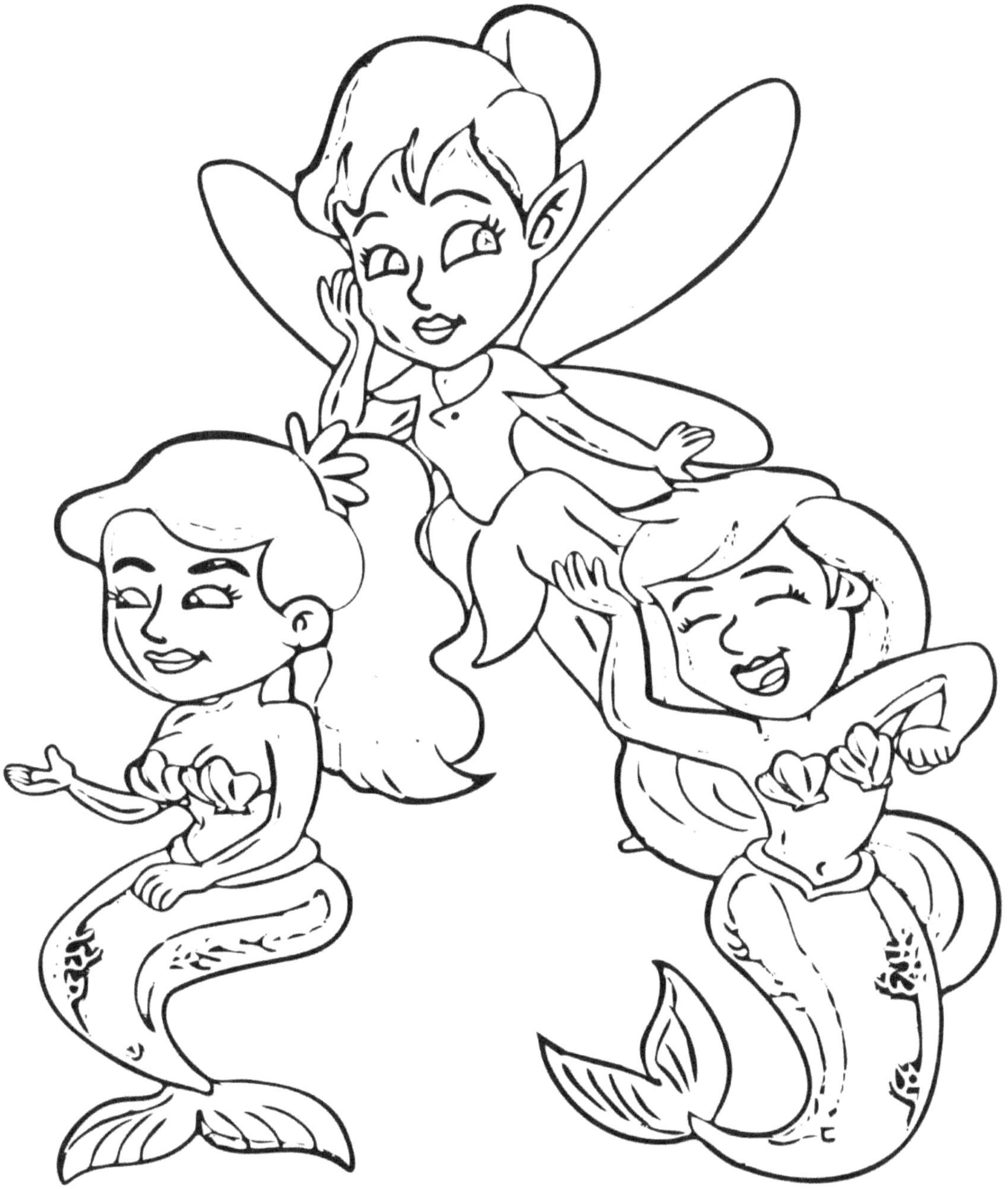

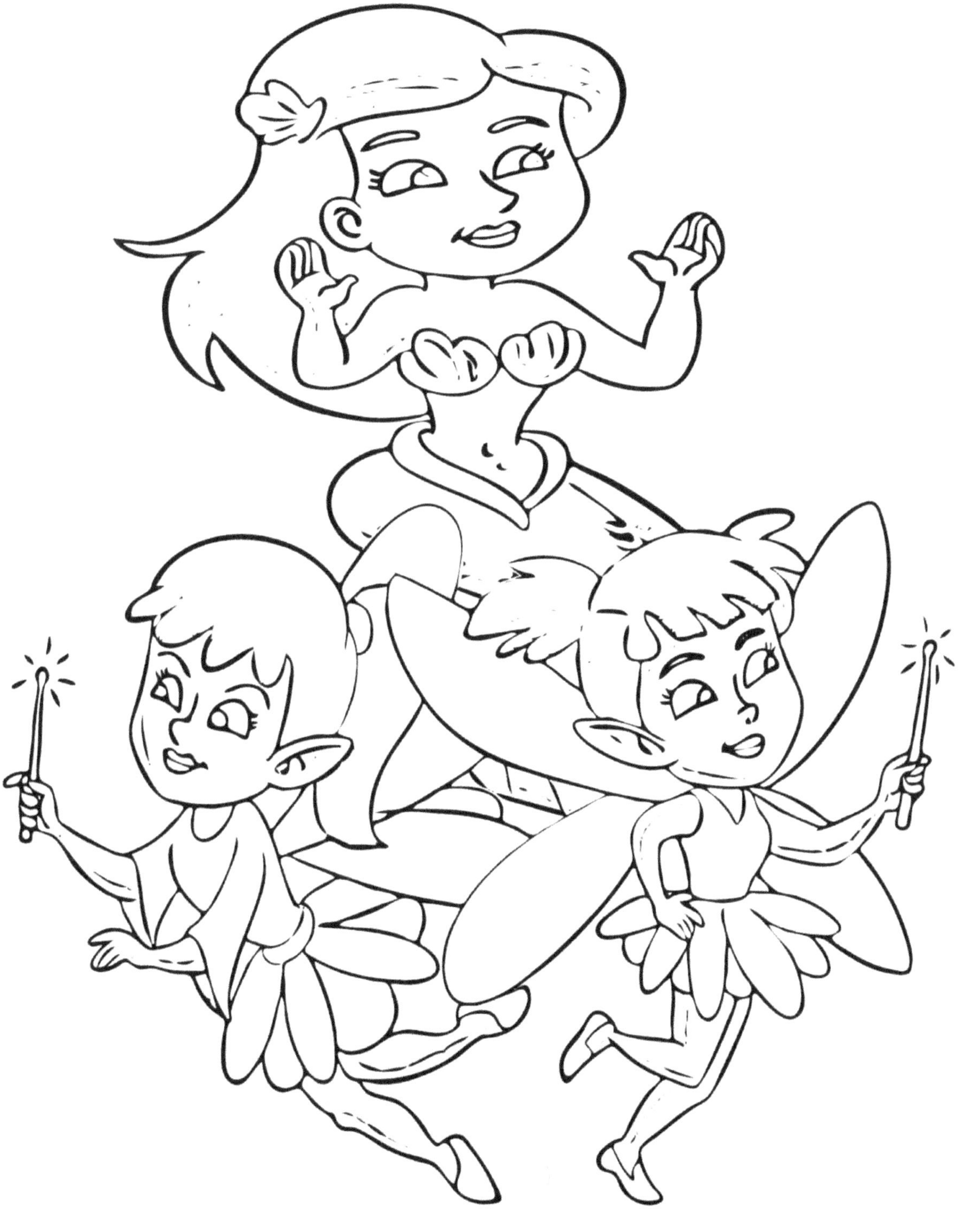

CREATURES of the SEA

Coloring Book

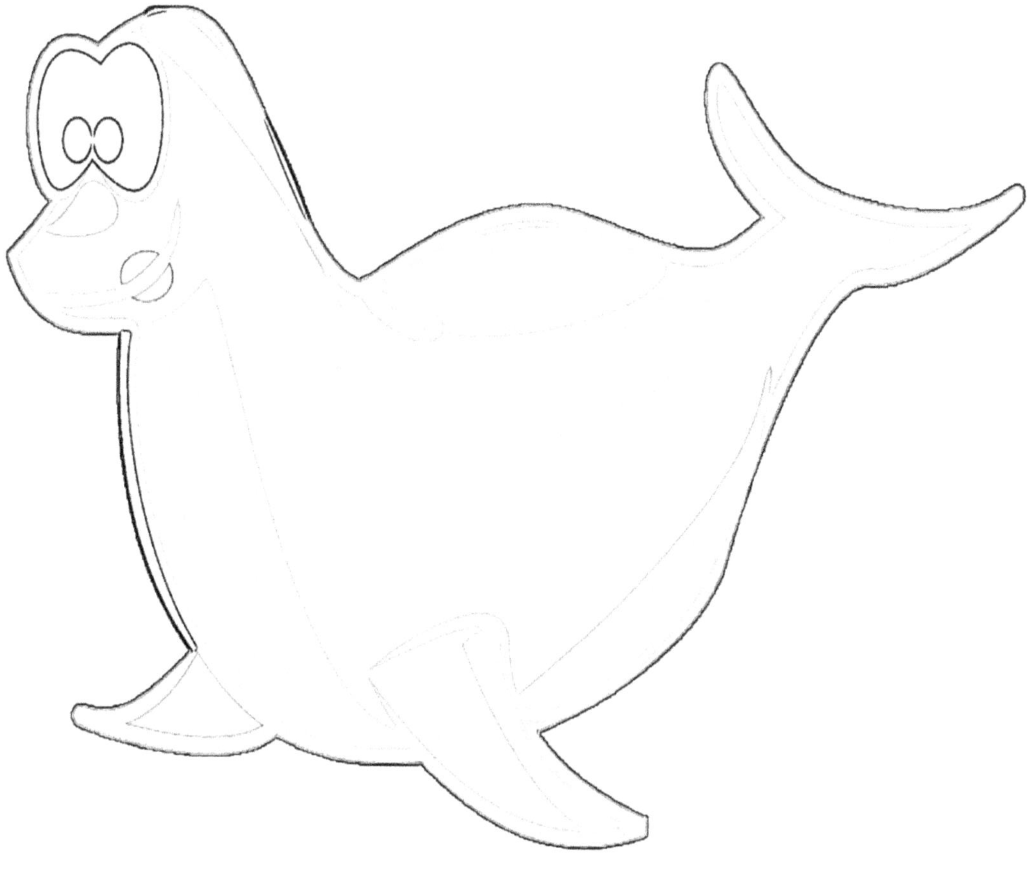

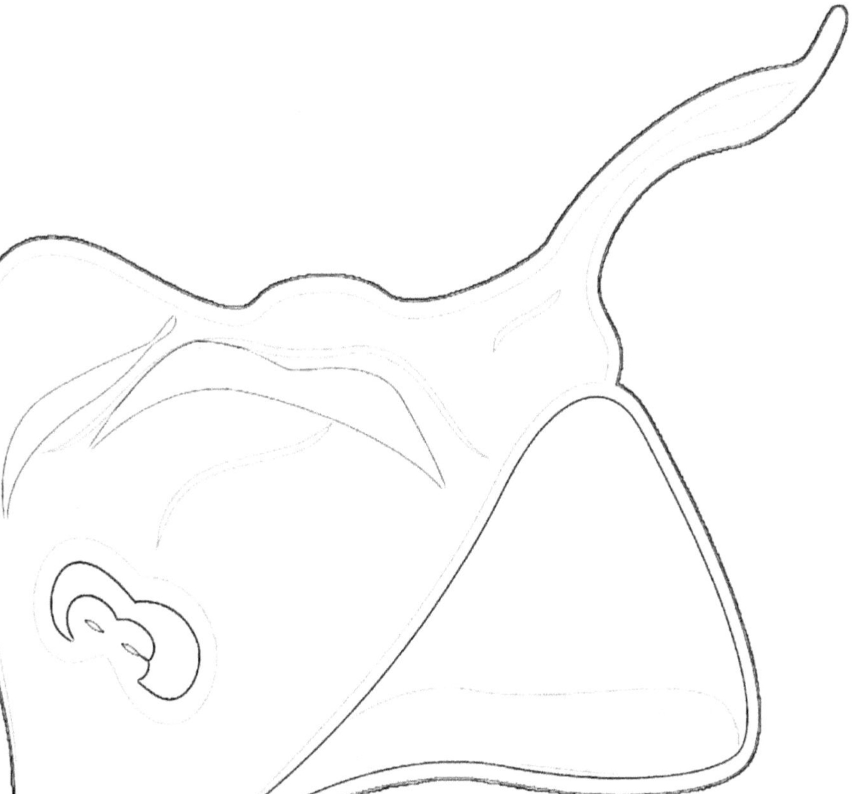

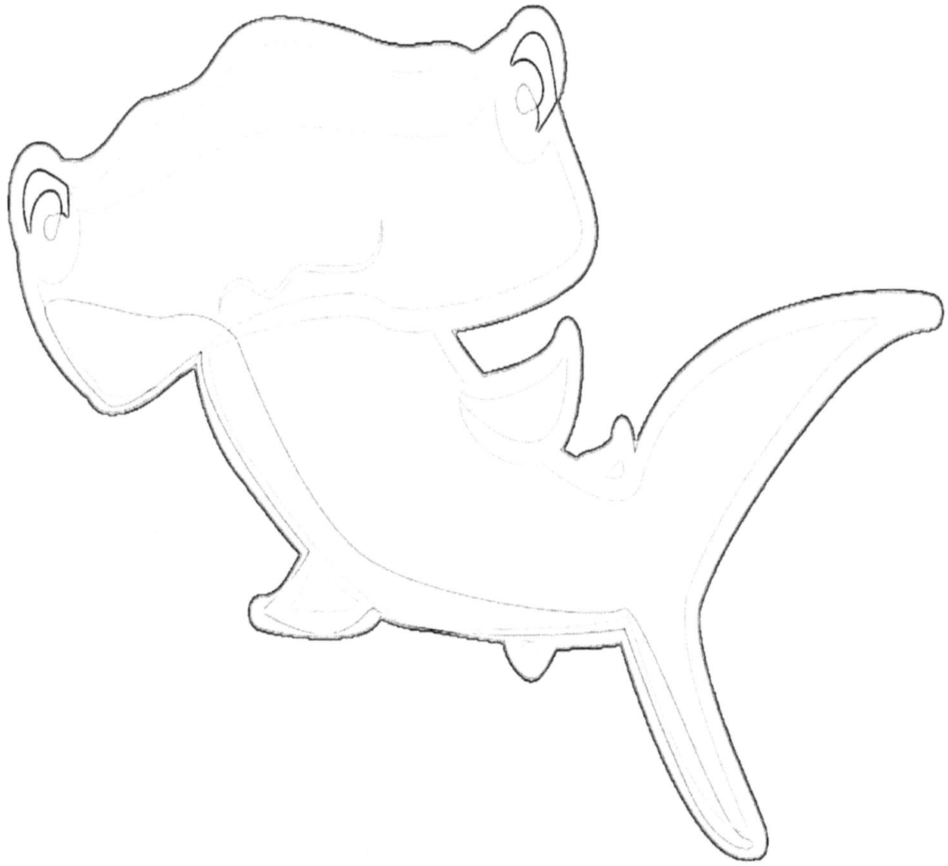

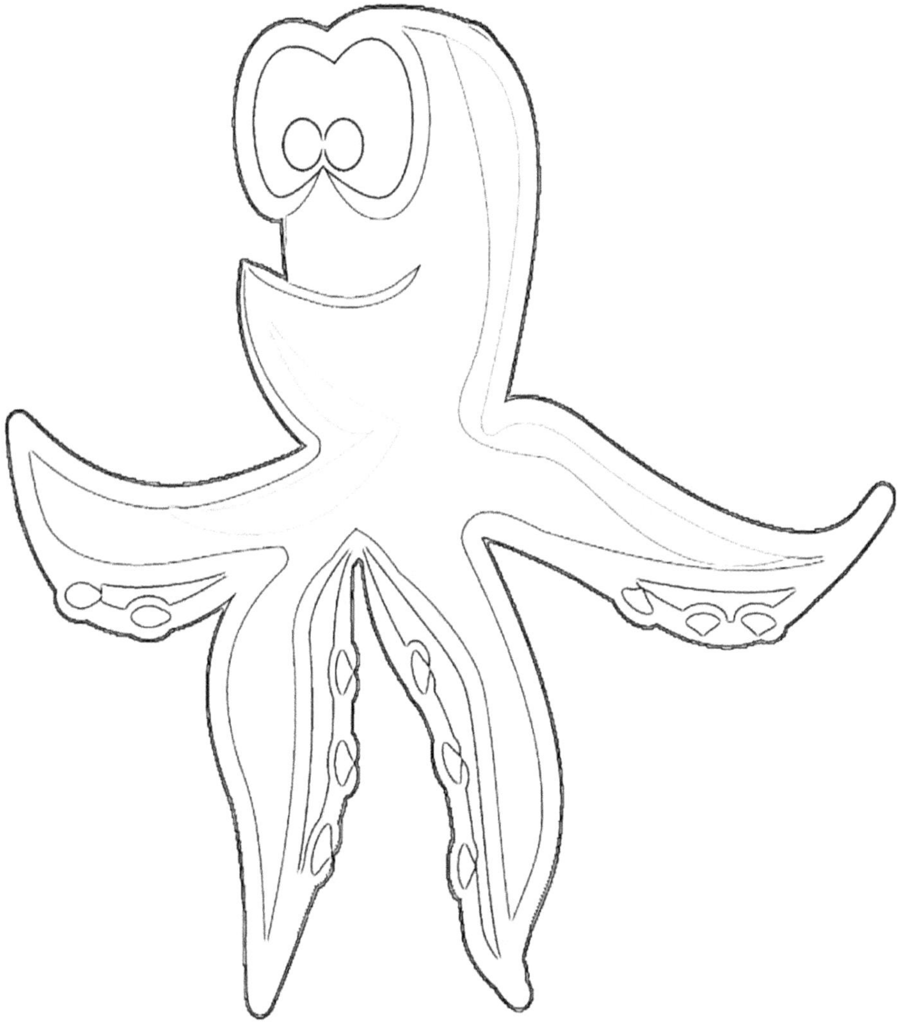

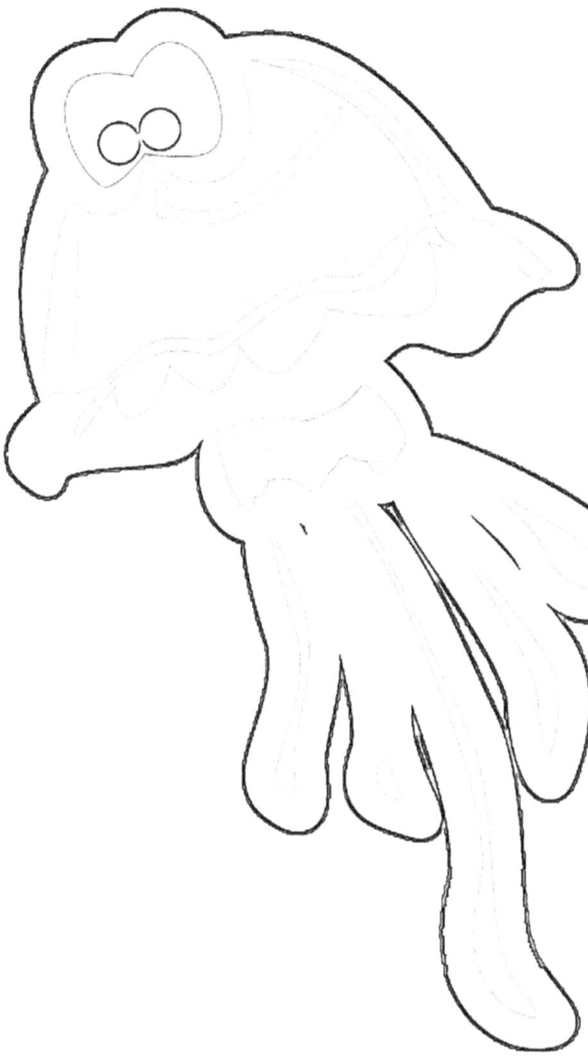

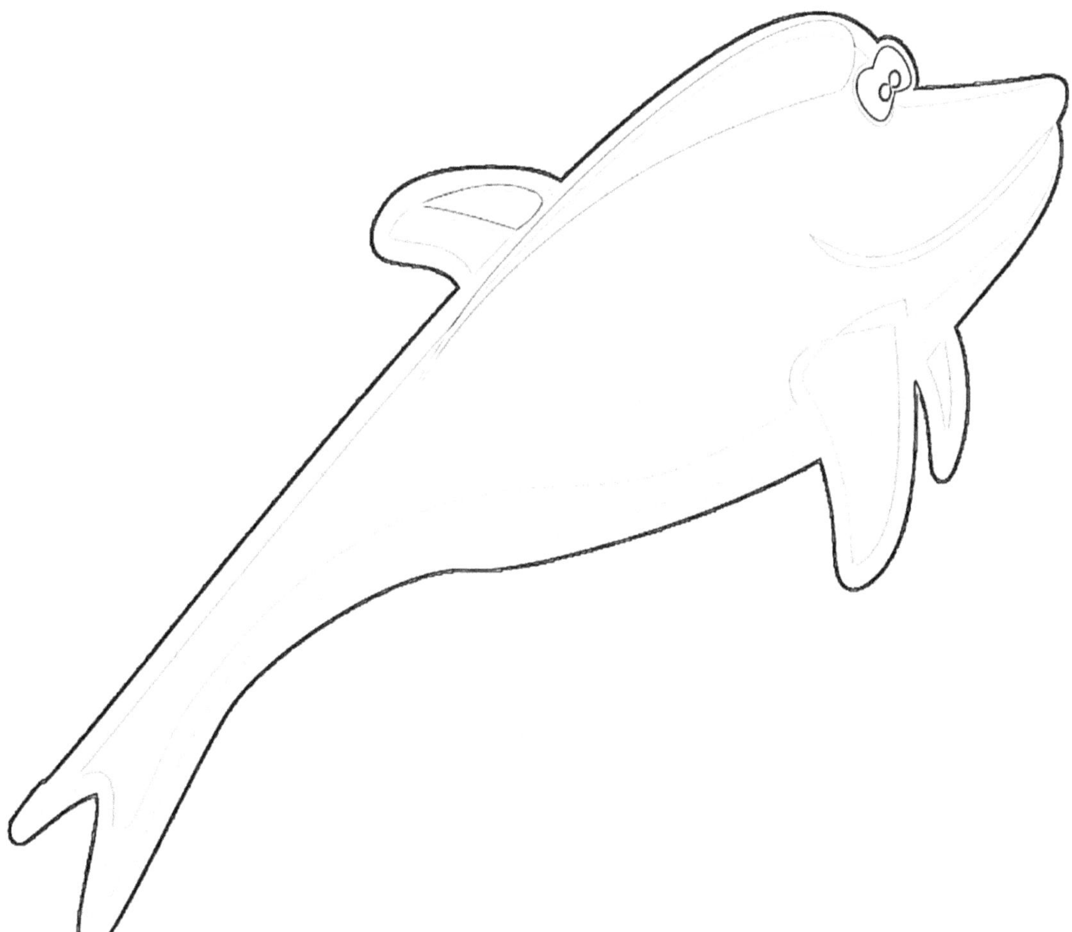

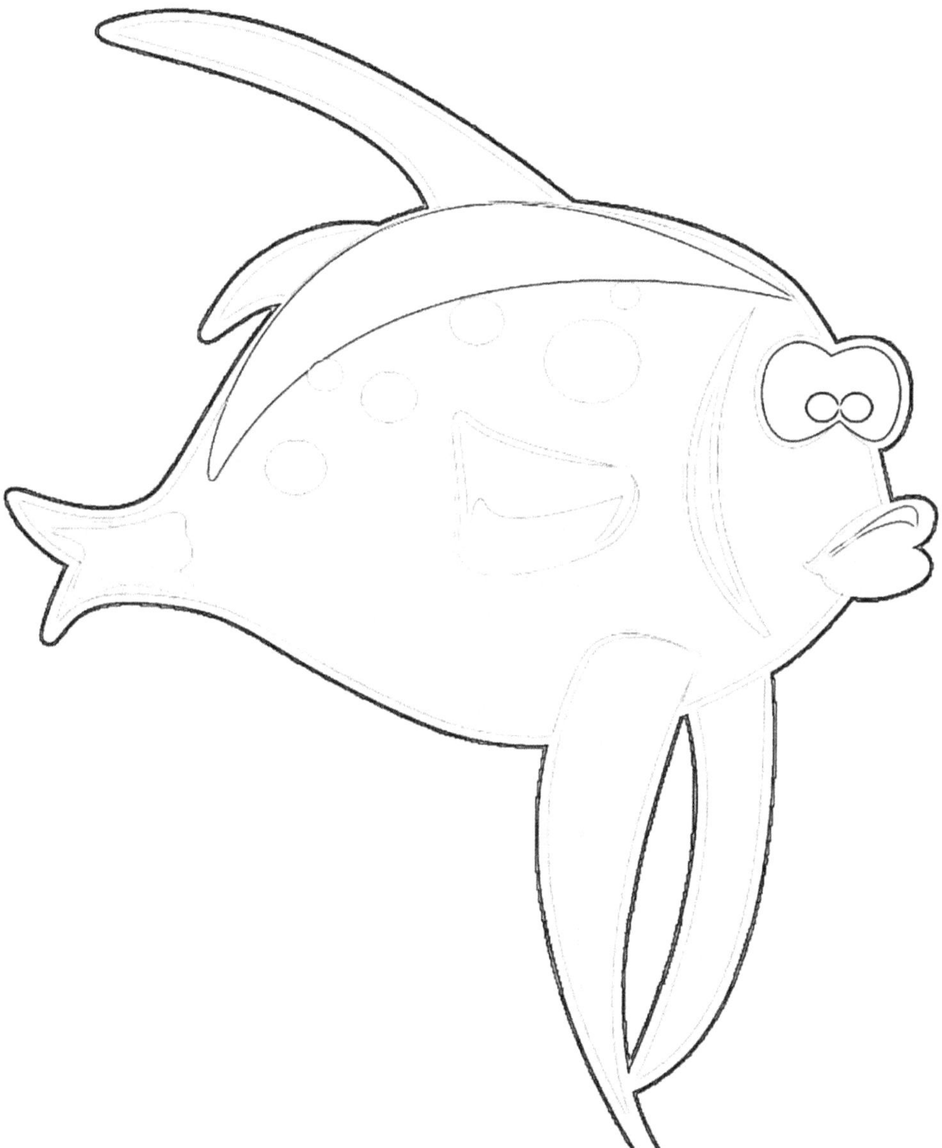

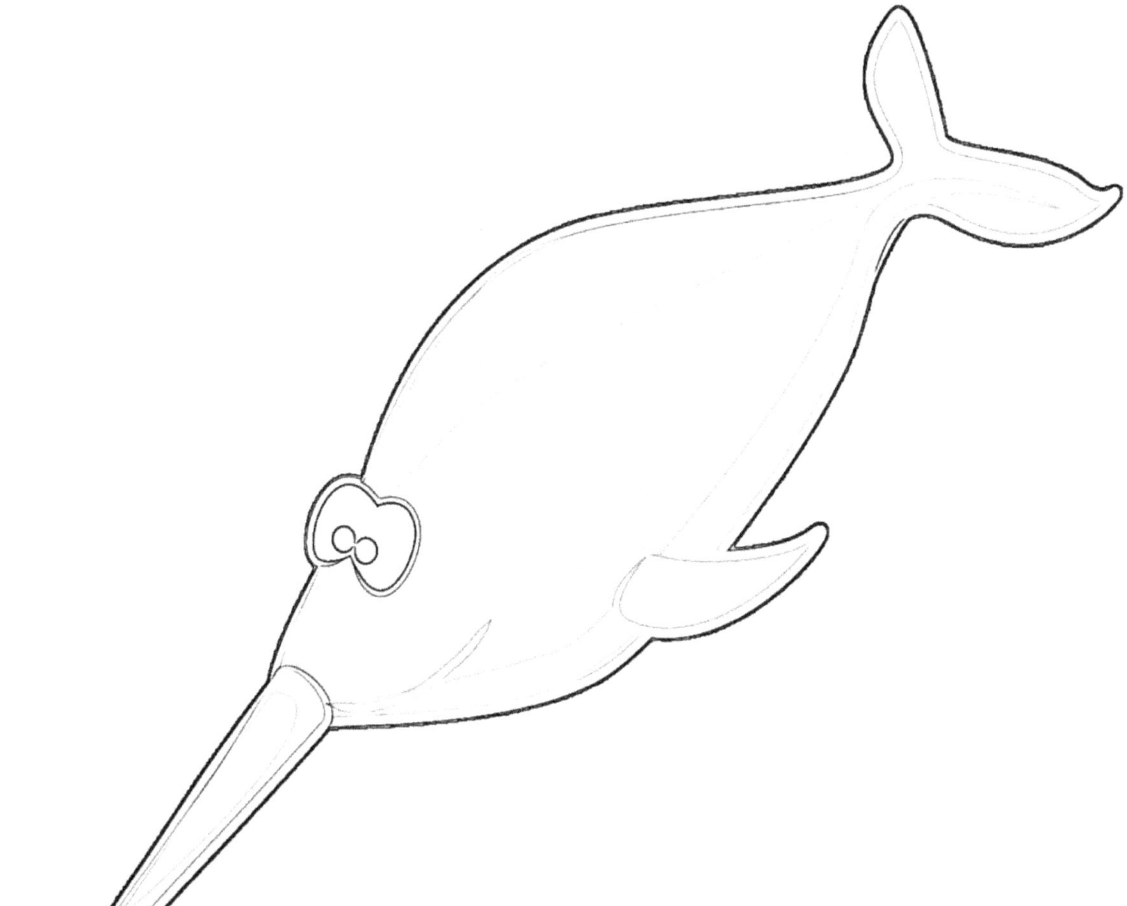

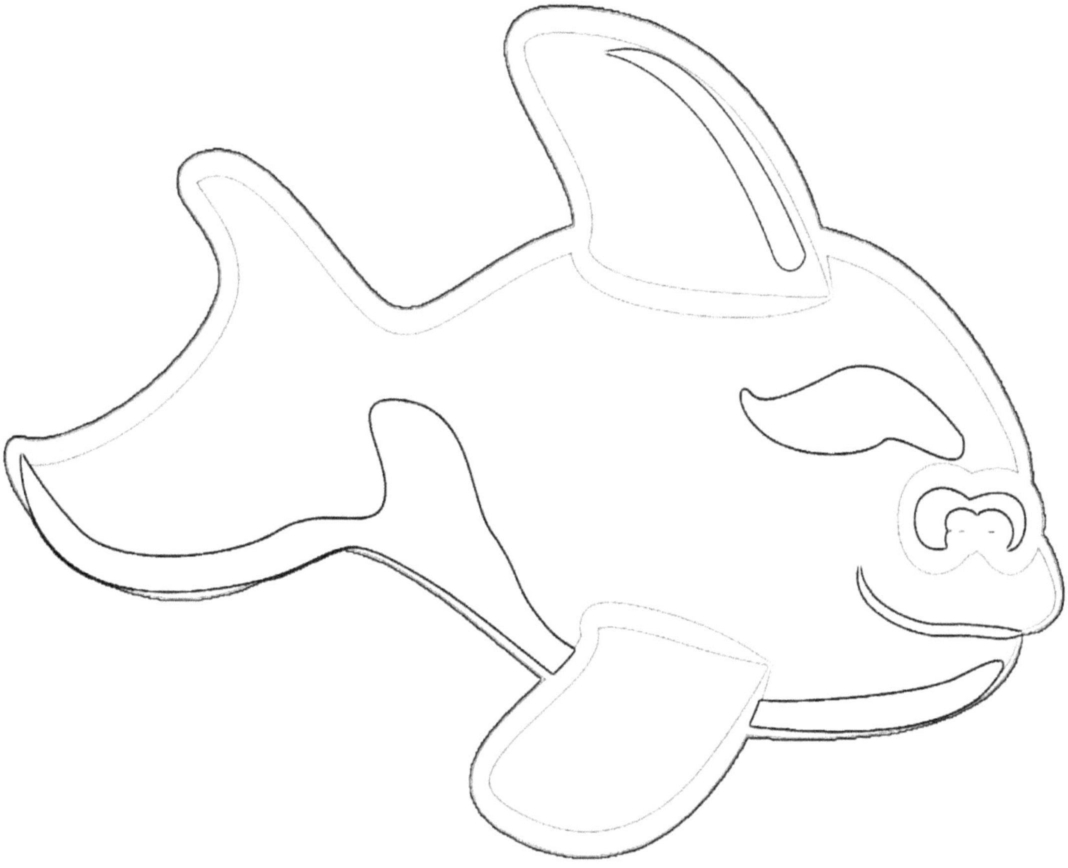

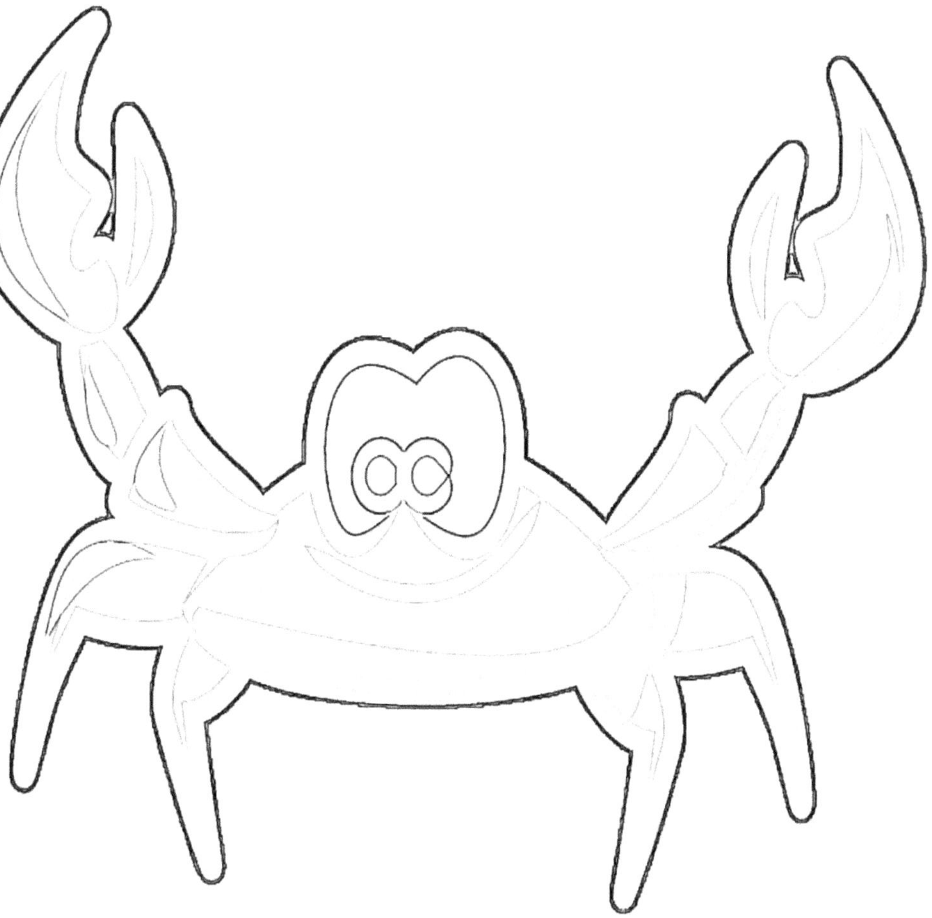

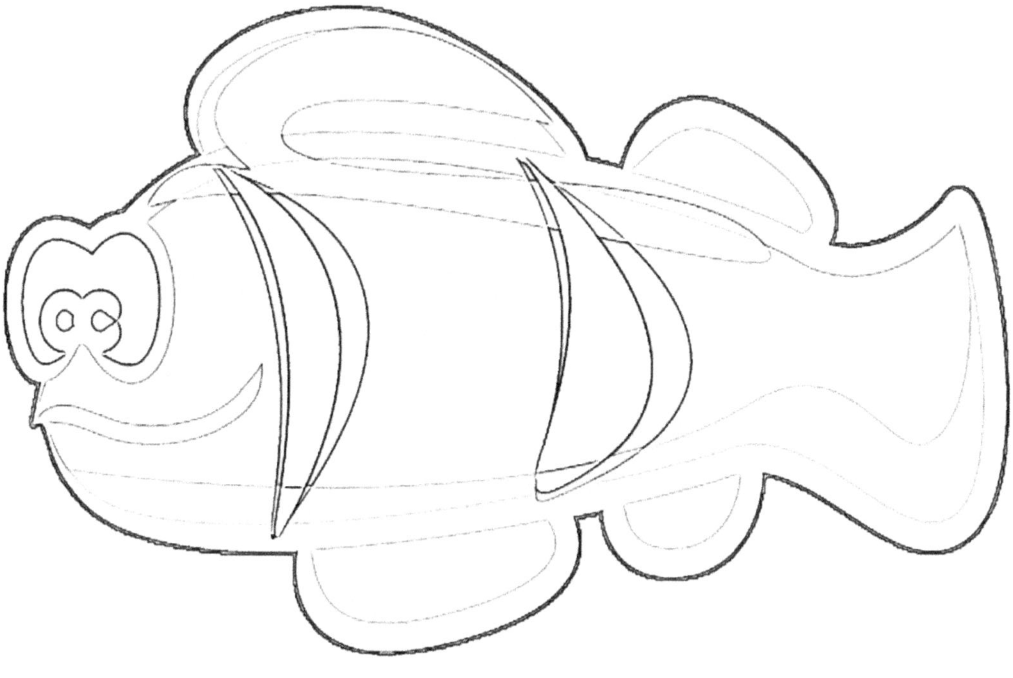

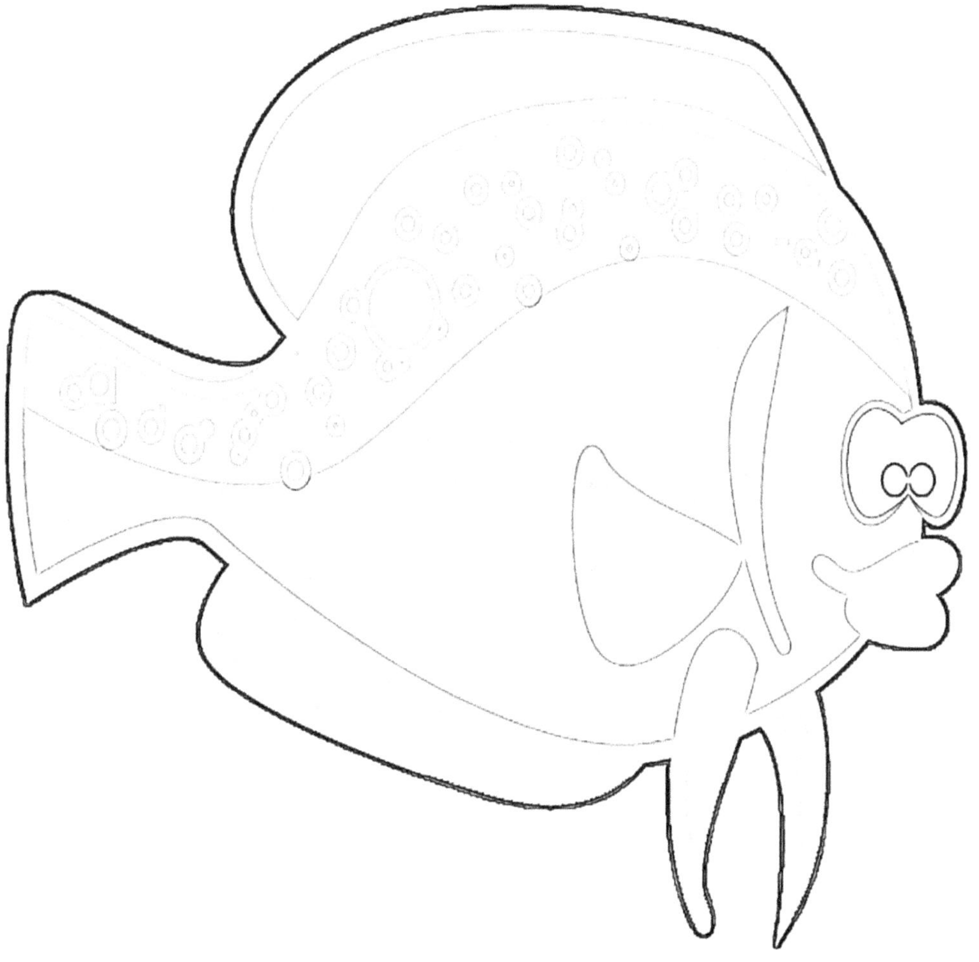

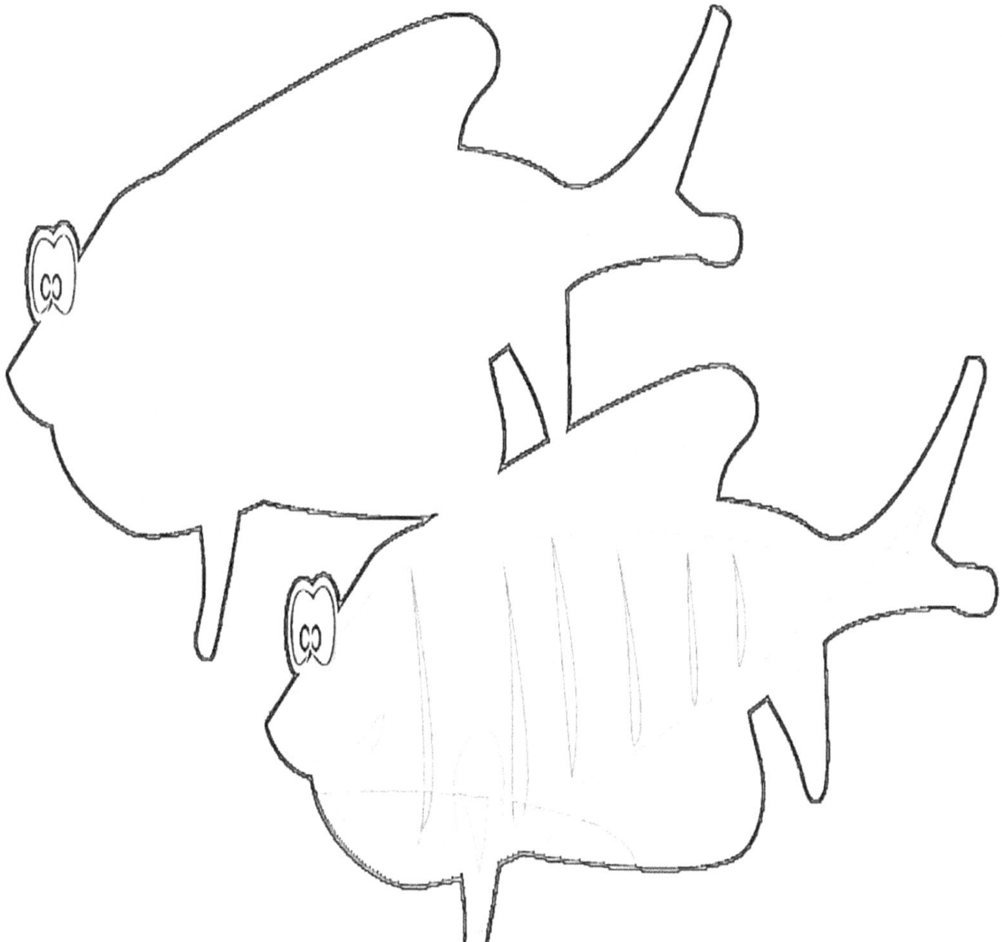

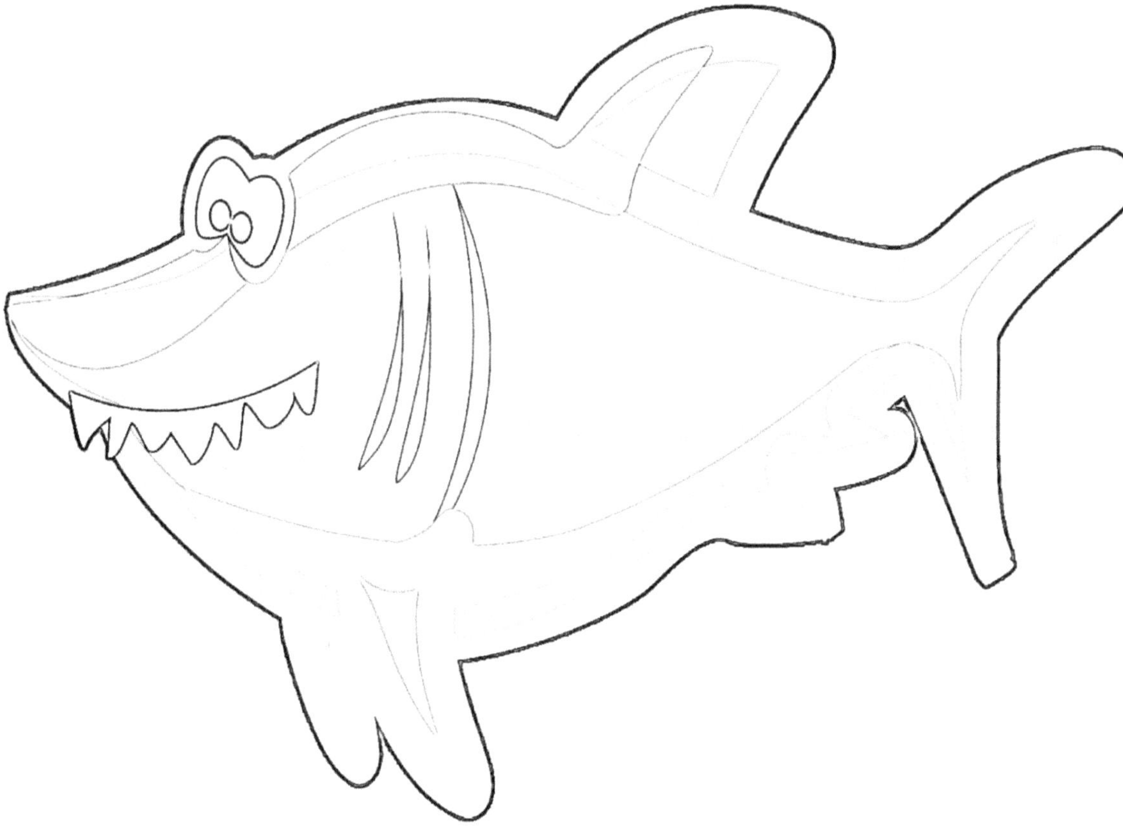

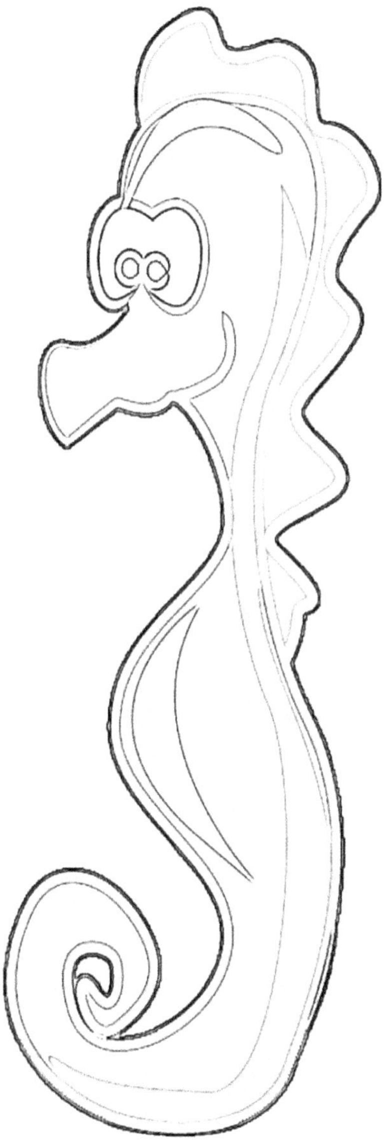

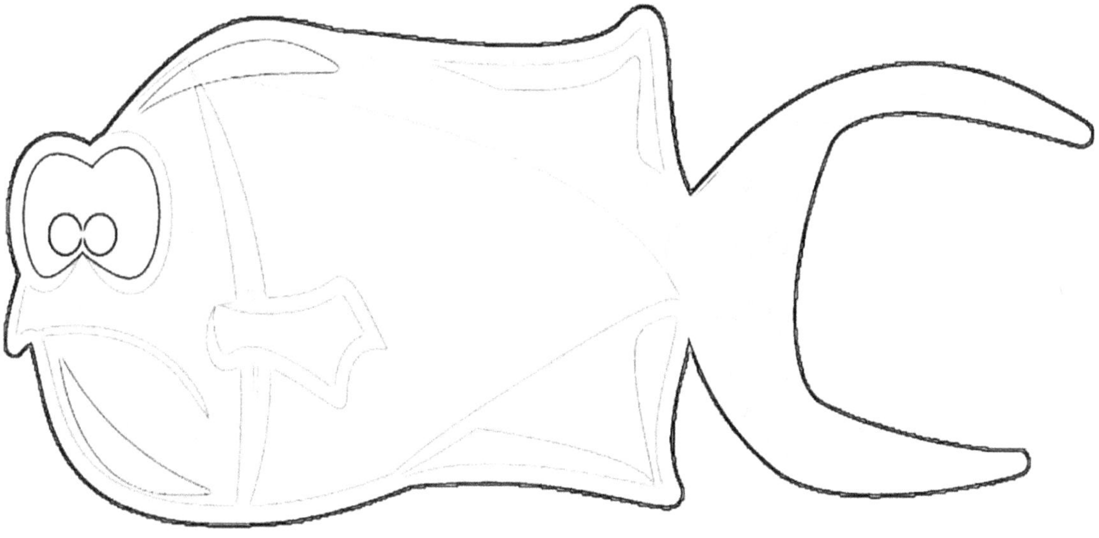

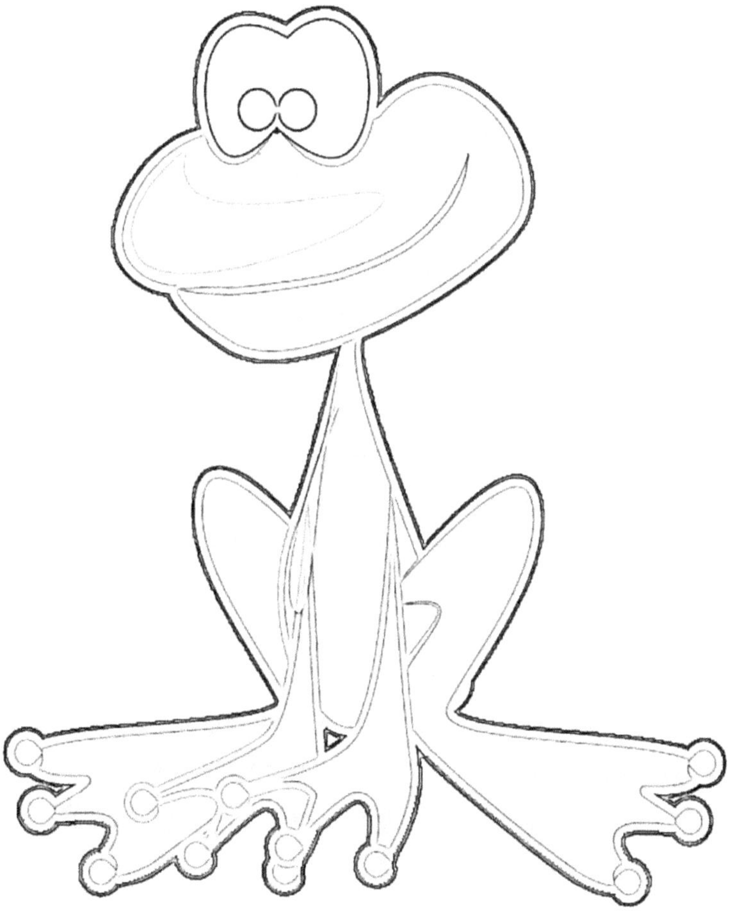

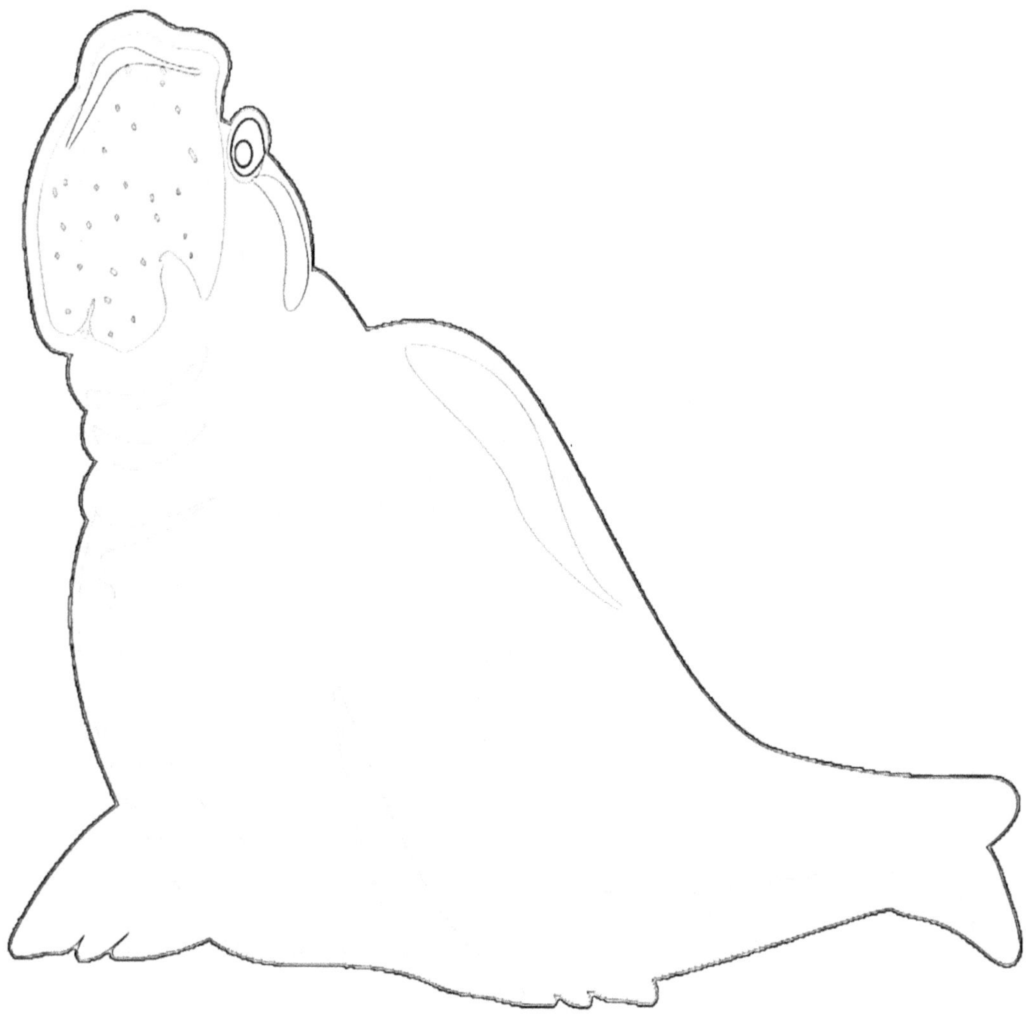

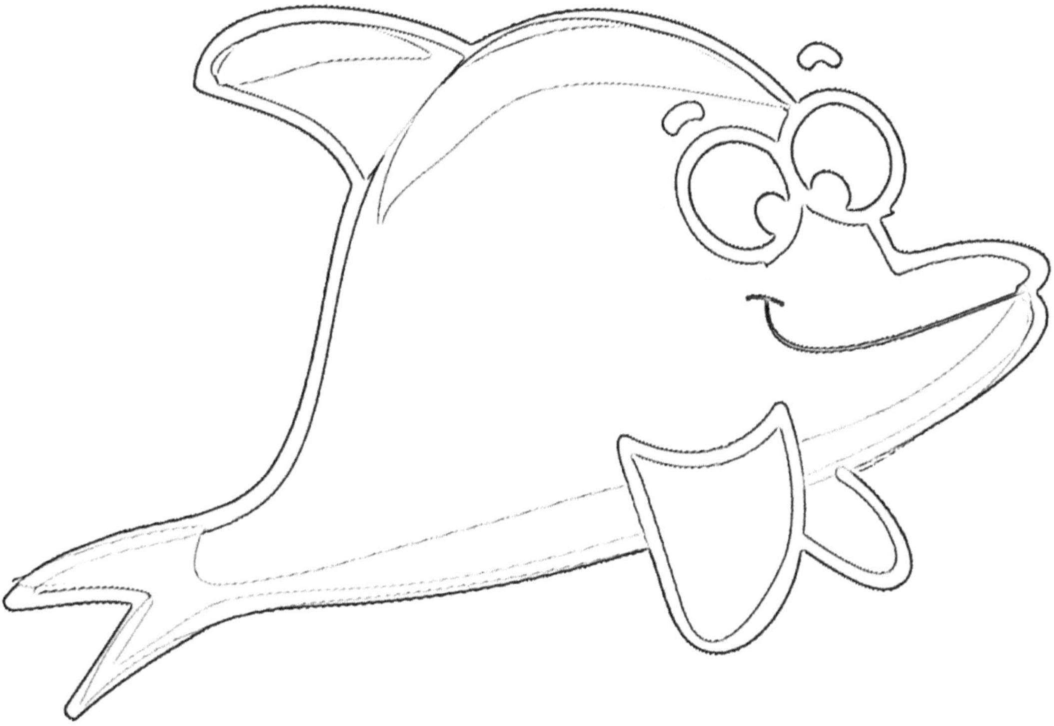

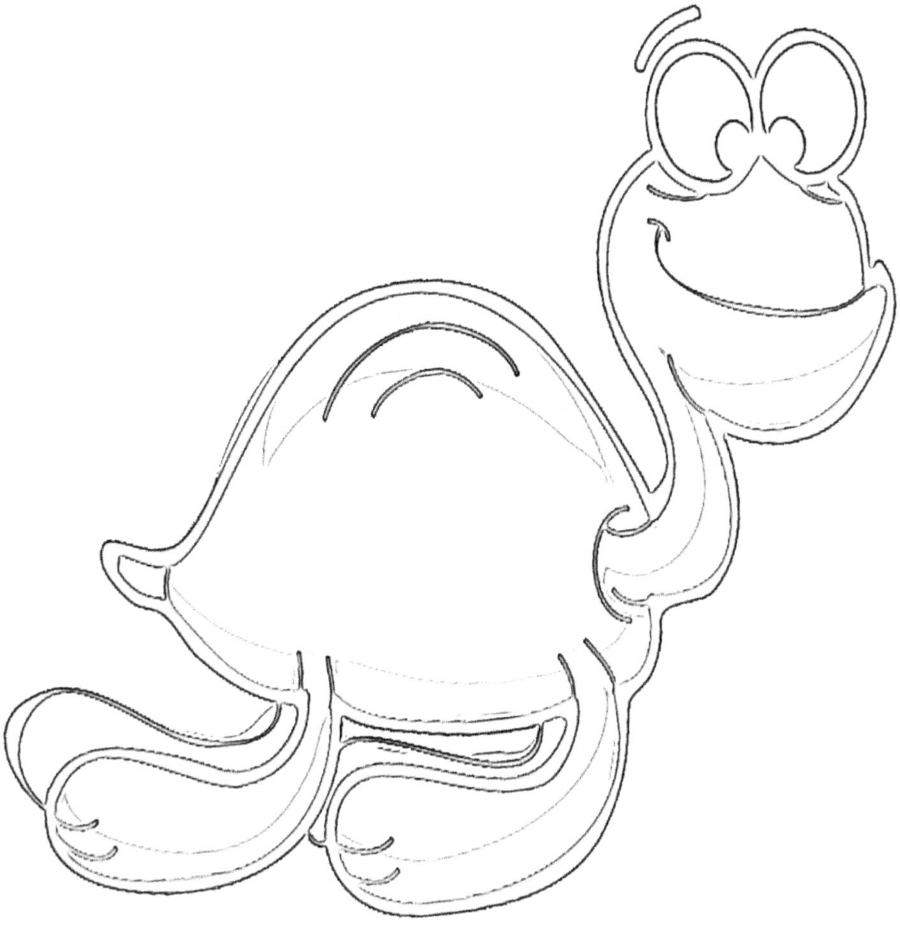

www.ingramcontent.com/pod-product-compliance
Lightning Source LLC
Chambersburg PA
CBHW081553170526
45166CB00009B/2681